THE DALAI LAMA SPENDS THE NIGHT

THE DALAI LAMA SPENDS THE NIGHT

and Other True Tales of

Despair, Hope, and Spiritual Transformation

CHRISTI COX

Published in the United States by

Spiracle

Copyright © 2018 by Christine Cox

All rights reserved.

ISBN: 9781794077560

Contents

Introduction	7
The Dalai Lama Spends the Night	9
The Dalai Lama's Detective	23
Dalai Lama, Alias Groucho	27
Falling Apart	31
The Italian Guide	43
The Magician of Switzerland: Paul Brunton	58
A Good Man	71
Sin	75
The Spider Woman	81
Mother Meera and the Glow of Spiritual Glitz	91
Spoiled and Sulky	110
Meera: The Broken Engagement	112
Next	132
Speaking Up and Out	134
Be Here Now vs Be Bliss Sometime	142

Chased by Hell	147
Disability Blues, Blacks, and Greys	154
Old Anger	157
The Shaft of Light	163
Mr. Universe: Adyashanti	174
Surrendering to Old Age and Everything Else, Maybe	180
Afterword	186

Introduction

My search for the Holy—even though I didn't always call it by that name or even recognize it for what it was—has been part of my life since I can remember.

Long before the Dalai Lama and Mother Meera stayed at my house (not together, of course), and long before I had other close encounters with people wielding powers of some extraordinary kind, I had been wondering about the nature of this strange world I found myself in as a child.

Over the years my search has been visceral, petulant, greedy, persistent. Also intellectual, misguided, utterly guided, entertaining—and yet, despite everything, absolutely serious. Because, really, what could be better than getting a glimpse of the Answer to the existential mystery that is our lives?

Over the years I've wooed the Holy, entreated it, created seductions of all kinds. I've invited the Divine to be my protector, my lover, my private standing army. (Of course, most of these invitations were blundering and inept.)

I've studied. I've meditated. I've tried. I've tried not to try. I've been blitzed by light, and by dark.

My dark has sometimes taken the form of one serious illness after another. Malfunction can be an effective attention-getting device from the Holy. Death, bless his black heart, is a very fine motivational speaker. The sharp blade of his sickle, nicking me even now, keeps me moving toward the spirit, toward myself.

Gradually I've learned about the various styles of spiritual courtship. I've come to see that I was going about it all wrong—or partly wrong. Perhaps, as with anything involving love and longing, a learning curve (or zigzag) is inevitable—as it is for all of us.

Through the extraordinary, puzzling luck of having spent personal time with the Dalai Lama, Mother Meera, Adyashanti, and other rare beings, I have some unusual stories to tell about these amazing spiritual leaders. My hope is that they will be useful, inspiring—or at least entertaining.

I share these linked true tales as a not-quite-memoir* of these encounters—with them and with my own obdurate, fragile psyche trying to find the Holy. It's a joke: the Holy is always unloseably here, of course. It just takes time to notice.

*Like all memoirists I practice the writerly arts of time condensation and of name/detail camouflage of some characters.

The Dalai Lama Spends the Night

My father laughed when I first told him that the Dalai Lama was going to spend a couple of nights at my house. Really, Dad, no kidding. Yes, that Dalai Lama. Tibet.

"If anyone had told me," he gasped, "when I was a young boy in Hungary, that I would have a daughter who..." Pulling a crumpled cotton handkerchief out of a suit pocket he daubed it towards his eyes, missing them completely. I'd never seen him laugh this hard before, but I knew he was a man who appreciated the absurd.

"...that I would one day have a daughter who might run bath water for a Dalai Lama...." He blew his nose percussively. "I would have thought they were crazy." He rotated his fingers expressively at his temple and rolled his eyes. He had experienced a lot in his life already. But this, this Dalai Lama thing, won the prize for implausibility. He shook his head, still laughing.

Barely a year into a marriage, my husband Jeff and I had recently resolved our décor disagreements—which mostly consisted of which hand-me-down furniture went into which room, and whether or not the weird metal eagle on top of a standing lamp could be sent to a suitable resting place in the village dump (yes). Things were livable; our various senses of aesthetics were reasonably appeased, considering. The fact that our house was new was a major plus, and a huge upgrade from our previous rat-infested, tippy-floored rental. So here we were, unsuspecting that both our lives were about to shift in unimaginable ways.

I was glad my rather old-fashioned father was pleased by this fresh news, the Visit. As for me, I wasn't sure what I felt. Puzzled, as though I'd just received a package from a foreign country where I knew no one, addressed to me in oddly familiar writing.

And truly, the fact that the Dalai Lama was coming to my house was extraordinarily unlikely.

First, I was not particularly a Buddhist. And he—of course—was the primary world Buddhist teacher. I was a messer-around in things spiritual, a curious wader in the spiritual life. Christianity, Hinduism, Buddhism, whatever, were all interesting, but none of them had seduced me into a deep plunge.

And second. Our house was located in the most economically depressed county in New York State, home to rusting cars abandoned in backyards. My neighbors lived in an alarming, corrugated metal building—and turned out to be the kind of people who shot each other. It was not an environment that most people would imagine to be appropriate for a dignitary of any kind, let alone an Eastern spiritual leader.

But he came. Looking back, it all seems like a scene from a quirky movie: the amiable sheriffs in the kitchen, the awful lentil casseroles I made for dinner, and the way I was broken out, or in, or up. Whichever preposition, it happened, and it changed the course of everything.

In 1979 the Dalai Lama had never been to the U.S.; he was not yet the familiar superstar he has become now. I'd never seen a TV story or newspaper article about him. In fact, I had no idea what the man even looked like.

All I knew was that he was an emblem of all that was still exotic and unknown in the world. And that somehow, some very unlikely how, he was coming over to spend a few nights as a house guest.

Harvard had been inviting the Dalai Lama for years, I was told. Weighty institutions of other kinds had also dangled invitations. That year, his first trip to the West, against all odds the Dalai Lama decided to visit a smallish group of my friends who were studying a variety of spiritual traditions in upstate New York. I did not yet know that when it comes to an influx of the Holy—in whatever form—"odds" has nothing to do with it.

A friend from our group had been contacted by the Dalai Lama's tour planner, who was on a mission to find suitable places for the spiritual leader to stay. This had turned out to be an unexpectedly difficult task: no decent hotels, not even upscale b&bs, within 20 miles.

The small house that my husband and I shared with our sweet, epileptic dog was merely one of the meager options in the area—with the advantage of being close to the rustic log buildings where our study group met.

The tour planner, remarkably enough, said he would come to check things out personally and then make a decision as to where to house the lama. At this point, it never occurred to me that the planner would actually choose my house. Why would he? It was so clearly not appropriate. Nor was I an appropriate host, shy and socially awkward as I was in those days. The Dalai Lama? Seriously? Here? I don't think so.

The planner turned out to be a charming, intimidating European sophisticate with impeccable manners and an appreciable amount of exhaustion. Because this was to be His Holiness's inaugural U.S. trip, he wanted everything to be perfect, but being a Buddhist and a realist, he knew that would be impossible.

After a surprisingly quick, discrete examination of our house, he suggested that His Holiness might indeed like to spend a few days of rest there. Perhaps his exhaustion had worn him down; I don't know. But it was to be. It was ridiculous. It was absurd. He told me, smiling slightly, that I had a few months to prepare.

It's obvious that the outer sequences of events that brought the Dalai Lama to the guest room of our house don't add up. The mathematics is off, doesn't seem quite sound. Why would a trip planner decide to house a world-class spiritual leader in a house like this? It made no sense then; it makes no sense now. The facts followed the logic of myth rather than that of any kind of Western science: the miraculous manifests inexplicably out of the void into a small, unlikely structure. It seems that's just how grace works. Always did; probably always will.

In anticipation of the visit I began to clean my house—seriously, absurdly, endlessly. Armed with a crisp toothbrush I vigorously scrubbed all my plastic spice boxes, and then—in a fit of utter irrationality—went on to bleach the underside of the sofa. For months rectangles of sponge sprawled, ready for immediate action, on window sills in every room. Cleaning like this—actually any cleaning beyond the cursory tidying triggered by impending guests—was not my usual style: I had always been a devotee of the minimalist school of dusting. But now things had shifted: I had to scour, scrub, and disinfect, moved by something ineffable. Deep within me something was pushing me around, while my conscious mind couldn't quite wrap itself around the facts, let alone the possible implication of the facts. The Dalai Lama, really?

My father, on a weekend visit, watched me polish with bemusement. This was not the untidy child he remembered. This was an obsessive young woman who seemed to be going overboard on this cleaning thing.

"Do you think," he said gently, having followed me down the steep stairs to the basement, "that the Dalai Lama will care about your canning jars?"

He blew his nose loudly as he watched me wipe two years of basement dust off the metal tops of the jars. Of course I knew that what I was doing was not quite sane. The spiritual leader of Tibet wasn't going to march into my house and then demand a tour of my basement or ask to review my pots and pans.

Of course not. Even as I scrubbed, I suspected that I was acting out a kind of archetypal urge for purification, one that most often precedes a spiritual initiation. Over the years I had read some religious writings—both Eastern and Western–explaining that significant spiritual events are often marked by a symbolic outer cleansing. Baptism. Immersion in the Ganges. Sprinkling with holy water. I, however, had apparently been seized by a hapless, suburban cleansing ritual—purification by bleach and window cleaner.

My father gazed at me for a moment. He was careful not to show more than the most minor shade of worry, a momentary paleness, and then he smiled. I knew what he was thinking: After everything that he had been through in his life, this was nothing to worry about. A funny thing, a rather pleasing thing, an amusing tale to tell his friends. And the obsessive cleaning? A little bit crazy, but better than its opposite, perhaps.

What I didn't tell him was that I was feeling pretty strange. There was a persistent sense that I was about to die. A traffic accident, maybe. Something big was coming at me—I could feel it—and I just hoped it wasn't going to take the form of a large hunk of metal hurling at me at ungodly speed over the blacktop. There was no way I could have confided such feelings; my father would have hyperventilated secretly and nagged me to go to see a psychiatrist.

But back then, in the basement, he let the space between us float lightly. Besides which, he was kind of excited. He wanted to see the fabled potentate of an equally fabled Shangri-la almost as much as I did.

On a cool October evening, a month later, two rotund sheriffs sat comfortably in my kitchen. Nice guys. Local boys, born and raised in nearby Watkins Glen, home to Nascar racing. On their belts, small speakers had just boldly announced that The Person was on his way to our house, protected by one squad car. "Tie-bet," the roundest sheriff said, as he munched on a proffered oatmeal cookie, "that's in Africa, right?"

Immersed in a quick tutorial—I felt that it was important that these sheriffs know whom they were guarding—I wasn't quite ready when the doorbell rang. Shoving the last of the small sponges into a pocket, I wiped my hands against my best skirt and went to the door.

There was a maroon robe, a shaved head, and a pair of very serious black oxfords. Also a high-tech watch and jaunty spectacles. A hand reached for mine and grasped it firmly. And then there were the eyes. They locked into mine briefly, briefly, briefly. They released; the hand released. And the Dalai Lama walked past me into the living room.

Now, decades later, I still don't know how to explain what happened in that quick interchange. There was no blinding light, no profound insight into the nature of the universe, no visions of the future. But it was one of the most transformative moments of my life. One moment I was a woman with a sponge, the next I was a fully ecstatic woman with a sponge.

This woman stood in shock in the doorway. Gently, a young monk who had been standing behind the Dalai Lama touched her on the elbow. "Could you show His Holiness to his room?" he prompted softly. The housewifely necessities of the moment called me back into a minimal congruence with this body, this room, this man. I managed to lead the way down the hall and swing wide the door to the compact room where the Dalai Lama would sleep. He walked in, surveyed the new orange pillows, the new creamy curtains, the new brown sheets on the bed. "Good," he said, guttural and noncommittal, and closed the door.

The young monk was tapping me on the arm again. His Holiness needs another towel, he said, and something to eat. He could see I needed prompting. "He likes bagels best," he advised, "lightly buttered."

With that mechanical oddness of people who have experienced trauma or some profound inner dislocation, I rummaged in the freezer for bagels. I had been traumatized, wonderfully, deliciously, profoundly. It was trauma stripped of its pejorative overlay. Outrageous, positive trauma. Balancing the bagels on a plate, I negotiated through the crowd of sheriffs and monks arrayed throughout the house, knocked on the door at the end of the hall, and waited.

The young monk opened the door; I could see the Dalai Lama sitting back against the cushions on the bed. "Thank you," said the monk, but I was looking beyond him into the room. From the orange cushions an arm with a high-tech watch raised into the shining air, and waved.

That night, as I lay awake in a lumpy borrowed bed with Jeff sleeping beside me, I noticed that every cell in my body seemed to be involved in a rhythmic, celebratory dance, vibrating so energetically that sleep was impossible. But I didn't care. The sense of fulfillment was so extreme that it occurred to me that I could die without regret right there and then on the broken springs.

"Trite thought," I said out loud, and laughed because I did not need to forgive myself for it. Trite or not, it felt truer than almost anything else in my life. That cool, miraculous night I would have given my life for the Dalai Lama instantly, without question. I felt utterly transformed and utterly baffled. And, apparently, madly in love. What had happened to me? What had happened after I opened the door?

The next day, and the next, the ecstasy continued. Each morning—floating in the fire of it—I began my part in the tight scripting of the visit. I laid out the meals that had been prepared—according to schedule—by friends who brought them steaming and fragrant to the door. Chocolate cakes, cherry pies, and vast bowls of cashews and dried fruit displayed their allure shamelessly along the kitchen counter. I often observed the attendant monks succumbing eagerly and happily to the gustatory seduction. But what the Tibetan leader chose to eat—besides bagels—I don't know. This was because, after making sure that the food was where it should be, my husband, Jeff, and I usually left the house to give the visitors—and the Visitor—privacy.

After the meals, teams of my friends from the study group arrived in the best cars they could borrow to transport the Tibetans to the halls where His Holiness was scheduled to speak. And, in a piece of elegant choreography, other friends let themselves into our house to clean it and wash the dishes while the guests were away. It was heaven: I didn't have to hoist a broom or heft a sponge.

How homey and casual it was, despite the valiant organizing and planning. Just a group of friends, making it happen. Drawing straws for the plum jobs, such as driving His Holiness. Baking their best barley casseroles. Even doing the laundry. These monks had been traveling for a while and, of course, their robes needed a wash. There's always something intimate about washing someone else's clothes. And something wonderful about throwing several maroon robes—including one belonging to the Dalai Lama—into a washing machine. A sentimental friend, whose machine it was, confessed later that she kept the lint as a memento.

These days the Dalai Lama travels with several sets of men in expensive dark suits and gun holsters. When he gets in or out of his limousine, entire city blocks are closed down; when he stays in a hotel, brand new plates and silverware are required—not because he's fussy, but because his security detail is concerned about poisoning. At my house, way back before we all knew better, we managed with home-baked pie, ancient cups, and a few stalwart sheriffs sitting uneasily in the flowerbeds at night.

Three days passed and it was time for the entourage to move on. We drove through cool sun to the small airport where a private aircraft had been hired to take the Dalai Lama to the next stop. Stepping out of the car, he pulled his robe tight against the wind, shook each of us by the hand, and strode toward the puny plane that lay on the runway. His attendant was visibly unhappy. Only one propeller. So small. But the Tibetan leader bounded up the two steps, turned in the low doorway, waved buoyantly, and was gone.

I returned home. Returned to the clean house still laden with carrot cake and casserole. Took my collection of sponges and threw them in the garbage. Lay down on the bed with the brown sheets and orange pillows. And understood, for the first time, that from here on out, I was on my way to becoming...what? I wasn't sure; I just knew that miracle happens, and this world was no longer quite as lonely and incomprehensible as it once had been.

This event with the Dalai Lama was like being handed a pair of 3D glasses in the middle of a movie that you didn't know was designed for them. You slip them on in the dark of the theater, and then—with an aha—see that everything that has appeared double and confusing up to now is actually leaping out in the most astonishing ways towards you.

    This unsought and improbable event, the fact that a great spiritual being could precipitate out of the exotic world and into my depressed corner of upstate New York, showed me something that I'm pretty sure is true. It is this: The Holy seeks us out, comes looking for us, no matter which unlikely fragment of this world—in the largest sense—we inhabit. Well, it showed me that—but it took me a long, long time to really see it, let alone believe it. Let alone trust it.

Over a few days, after the Dalai Lama left, I began to put my house back into pre-Dalai order. The croissants and banana bread on the counter took a brief detour into the refrigerator and then onto the dinner table before landing around my hips. The piles of towels in the bathroom and several sets of sheets returned to the closet where they mingled with other bed linens that had not been so near to greatness. Even the zinnias in my garden began to recover from their close contact with the amiable sheriffs. Everything seemed normal. But actually it was oddly, delightfully abnormal.

    As I puttered and straightened, I could feel that the tectonic plates of my inner being had shifted irrevocably, deep below the fragile constructions of my psyche. When the Dalai Lama took my hand and looked into my eyes, he'd changed me so profoundly that I couldn't yet suss out the exact nature of the change. But it was undeniable: I knew that I was an amended person. Most of the transformations I'd experienced in my life before—and there were many—were pick-and-axe work compared to this seismic shift—or so I thought. And there was the undeniable facthood of the bliss, which effervesced mildly for about a month, and then faded quietly away.

There are fulcrum points in a life, ones we use as markers of significant change. A fall into love, a diagnosis, a birth of a child, a certain job, a divorce, a realization that we're not immortal after all. Sometimes the change is slow-mo; and other times it is so acute and unexpected that the glue of our world softens, and it's unclear who and where we'll be when it hardens again.

The first, slow signs of the extent of the change began when—almost immediately—I found myself sketching imaginary deities in the margins of my books. Deities emanating light. In other words, deities sporting halos.

The mysteries of halo-depiction consumed me. How can one capture something that is as much experiential as visual? Just how large should halos be? And exactly what color? And why?

Right from the beginning it was clear to me that my (mercifully brief) obsession with these drawings was simply a small, outer sign of my new internal configuration. But inner or outer, all of it was an effect of the zap, the whap, the wallop, the whatever that the Dalai Lama had given me that night.

And I kept wondering: What had that man done to me anyway? And how did he do it?

The experience left me ruminating on the nature of sudden exaltations—the ones you get from being near spiritually developed people. Did they last or were they just very pretty flashes in the pan? Pretty flash or true flame, I wanted to find out more. Of course I wanted another hit of something that felt that good. I was greedy and I was curious—a good combination for getting into new kinds of trouble. Good trouble, even virtuous trouble. But did it take me closer to the Holy? Maybe, maybe not.

The Dalai Lama's Detective

Some years after the Dalai Lama's visit, rummaging through my closet to find the perfect aqua sweater to counteract the grayness of a mood, I found the pillow case used by the Dalai Lama when he stayed over, neatly folded up in a plastic bag. I'd kept it, unwashed, as a talisman against disasters I was sure would eventually show up.

I always expected disasters. From my parents—survivors of various traumas— I had learned all too well that the world was deeply dangerous. A large tractor trailer might be racing towards me. Or a deadly disease. Or the kind of knock at the door that you don't want to hear.

Holding the pillow case against my cheek, I checked into my expected-disaster meter. It was relatively quiescent. But there was the usual, banal discontent. It barely needed excavation—it was twitching visibly, barely below the surface.

At the first level, hardly covered by dust, was my usual state of wanting things to be different.

I could see that at almost every moment, habitually, I placed a petition with the deity: Wanted, fewer wrinkles. Wanted: no headache. Wanted: a large piece of chocolate ganache, stripped of caloric implications.

It was a kind of spoiled-brat discontent of the most uninteresting kind. The Buddhists say this is what keeps us miserable—our refusal to accept the moment as it is, with its saggy jowls and calories, its migraine and endlessly ringing phone. Most of the pain is not in the head or the eye bags; it's in the petulant rejection of the head and eye bags. We are always wanting what we don't have and fending off what we do.

Even if we manage some gratefulness for this or that, there's almost always some picky thing that we'd rather was different– bigger, smaller, prettier, sunnier, tastier, richer, greener, or spicier. Kvechiness apparently abhors a vacuum.

"You idiot," I said to myself, trying to pull myself out of my pathetic state, "you know better." And I did.

Putting the pillow case back on its top shelf shelter, I kvetched to myself about the ever-presence of kvetchiness, polluted myself about the ever-presence of self-pollution. And so it went.

And that's when I first saw Detective Mike Davis. Sick of my mood—and prompted by the presence of the pillow case—I decided to look at an old unedited videotape that had been shot during the Dalai Lama's visit to Cornell. I'd borrowed the tape to research the Buddhist leader's speech at that event, but once the video started, I immediately got quite distracted by an image of an elegantly attired university detective, awkwardly answering an off-screen interviewer. His name was apparently Mike. He was sweating in a fine suit, his dark skin damp against the improbable crispness of his shirt.

I should confess here that I fall into the ficklest kind of love easily and often. These are the ten-minute loves, evoked by the bits of astonishing beauty that just about every human carries: the subtle green of a sharp mind, or a wicked scarlet humor, or an unusually tender kindness that seeps through a stern face. Still, I was surprised by my reaction to Mike.

"My position in this detail was to help secure the location," he began. He was a professional, a protector, a police officer. "I knew very little about the Dalai Lama. I thought it was going to be another dignitary visiting basically to promote his cause. But I was wrong."

He paused and then looked directly at the camera. "I thought I'd be involved in making his stay comfortable and safe; I never thought that he would make *me* feel comfortable and safe."

Now he had my attention, but not yet my love. But then he said it. "The Dalai Lama affected me in a very, very strange way. He made me smile so much—I'm not a great smiler," and the most radiant and humorous of smiles broke through the control of his face. I was enchanted. Mike attempted to restyle his face into the demeanor he thought suitable for a law enforcement officer, but it was hopeless. His beauty was in control.

"He's powerful," he said quietly. "And when I say powerful, I really mean powerful. When he touches you, you know you've been touched. He shakes your hand and you feel it in your toes and it bounces back in your heart. You say *geez, what just happened*." I jumped up excitedly from the maroon futon facing the TV.

"When he touched my shoulder once in the elevator, it was a good thing I was standing next to the wall," the officer continued. "It didn't look like he was doing anything but I felt it all the way to my toes. It was amazing. It was awesome. He's a different type of person."

I turned off the video and reached for the phone. It wasn't difficult to find Mike; it turned out he was still a detective at Cornell.

He was guarded on the phone: alert, professional, crisply monosyllabic. But when I said that I wanted to talk to him about the Dalai Lama, I could hear him surface into the light. In fact I could almost see the smile of a man who is not a great smiler. "Wow," he said. "In a word, wow." He promised to call me back, after I suggested he might like to see the video, but he never did. I was disappointed, but somehow felt shy to pursue him. Besides which, I was already out of love.

But again I wondered at that strange, potent force that can move through spiritually advanced beings, affecting people—like Mike—whose world view doesn't include the possibility of such a thing happening. What does the experience do for/to someone? Is it just a spiritual Twinkie, fun but ultimately unnourishing? Or does it change one, irrevocably?

The Dalai Lama, Alias Groucho

My friend Sid once strategically placed Groucho glasses—complete with nose, bushy eyebrows—in a hotel room where the Dalai Lama would be staying during his visit to Cornell University. Sid's sense of humor is usually of the low-burner variety, warm in the background, but not often flaring in risky directions. So the Groucho thing was a brave gesture because, really, who could gauge the terrestrial and spiritual consequences?

And it was also a gesture of friendliness, because His Holiness had once told Sid that always having to be the Dalai Lama didn't give him much freedom. Being both a spiritual and a political leader is a 24/7 job with a lot of responsibility and not much room for play.

Sid, being a gentle and compassionate man, wanted to help. A disguise—humorous and absurd—he thought, would be just the thing.

In the years between the Dalai Lama's first local appearance and this one, Sid and Jeff had become the owners of a publishing company, Snow Lion Publications, focusing on all things Tibetan: religion, history, culture. I worked there too, as an editor, sporadically. This, obviously, was one of the ways our lives had been transformed by the Dalai Lama's visit. As a result we were often involved in Dalai Lama-related events.

As one of the main organizers for His Holiness's visit to the campus, Sid was in charge of making sure that the suite was suitably equipped. Thoughtfully he placed an antique Buddhist statue next to the bed and Groucho on the bathroom counter.

So imagine this: a small cascade of university bureaucrats arrayed in the Dalai Lama's suite, waiting to meet the great man. They sit erect in armchairs designed for slouching. They're keyed-up by the barricade of media flacks surrounding the hotel, the barricade of FBI men surrounding the suite, the barricade of fear—they have spent inordinate amounts of donor money on this visit. And they, like all humans, harbor the deep longing to be knocked back, up, out by an influx of spirit and greatness.

Minutes pass and then a door flings open. Unaccountably, Groucho Marx— wearing maroon robes and serious lace-up shoes—emerges, chuckling loudly. Laughing so hard that tears come to his bespectacled eyes.

Would most people in power—our religious leaders, our politicians—do something like this? Not likely. We Westerners like to think of ourselves as witty and irreverent—and on the whole we are. But there's a line over which we don't cross—and that's ourselves. Oh, sure, we're big on bits of charming self-mockery, seductive gestures of self-deprecating humor, but only to the degree that we don't damage the way we're evaluated by the world. It's containment, not modesty.

Would any politician meet a foreign dignitary wearing something that suggests that really, when it down to it, we're all a bit of a joke?

Although by this time I had become familiar with Buddhist thought, there was something about the Dalai Lama's Groucho episode that really brought a small facet of the teachings sharply into focus for me.

Buddhism's bottom line is to be free of the domination of the ego—the need to affirm it, plump it up with collagen. It is being unconcerned about whether or not you're seen as a hot-shot Dalai Lama or a hot-shot editor or parent or even a half-way decent anything. It means not being jerked around by the need to look as good as possible, to others and to yourself. The ego is just a construct. Get over it.

Not so easy, of course. Certainly not for me.

One ancient, wizened Tibetan lama I had met—revered as a great meditation master—would occasionally hide a whoopee cushion in his guest chair. You can imagine. You're about to confess the *sturm und drang* of your inner life to the wise man. Or maybe you're interviewing him for an article. You lean forward and suddenly a loud fart bellows from the region of your buttocks. Perhaps it's a test; perhaps it's a joke; perhaps it's you. Do you despair or laugh or what? Go into shame: that's what I do.

Being my own spin doctor is a losing battle. I was never very good at it, but my ego continues to try—valiantly, hopelessly, stupidly. I don't want to wait until I'm raving or incontinent with dementia to start letting go of that compulsive attempt to keep the product of my ego as marketable as possible. But it's so, so hard to stop.

Back then, in the Ivy League hotel suite, the Dalai Lama didn't care about positioning his Dalai product-line. He saw a chance for fun, for deflating others' expectations, and he took it. And he just somehow knew whom to thank. Wagging his finger at Sid, he took off the mask, still laughing.

Falling Apart

Although my encounter with the Dalai Lama was a game-changer in many ways, I'd already been in various kinds of non-monogamous spiritual involvements for years before he showed up.

In fact, by the time I met the Tibetan leader I was a kind of sloppy Hindu-Zen-Platonist-Jewish-Christian-Sufi mix. I'm tempted to use the word *amalgam* instead of *mix*, but that implies a tighter bonding of the spiritual chemicals than I actually had. What I had was more like a kind of stew: chunky, disorganized, and fragrant enough to keep me going and reasonably nourished. The world's mystical systems all seemed to have such promise—for what I wasn't sure. Maybe peace, maybe truth, maybe something for which I didn't yet have a concept.

When the Dalai Lama came to visit, I'd been trying to meditate for a few years. I'd read sutras, tantras, Plato's dialogues, but had understood just a few of the ideas that floated up to my raft of a mind out of those books. When you're first searching for Divine Love, you're always looking around, because you just never know.

Looking for Love, yes. But—more honestly—it was an acute desperation and fear that was propelling me.

When I was a kid I hadn't yet figured out yet that a relationship with the Holy was desirable. It didn't help that St. Martins, the rather pretty Anglican church I was forced to attend as a child, was one of those who's-wearing-the-best-hat kind of places. My church in Sydney, Australia—which is where I grew up—was all about correct attire. Hundred degree weather or not, all females were required to wear white gloves, starched dresses, and hats.

Sitting alone in a hard pew each Sunday, I had no idea why I was there, except that my parents faithfully dropped me off by the puny shrubs at the entrance without fail every week.

There was something strange about this, but I was slow to pick up on it. And then one day I got it: other kids' parents actually went to church with them.

My parents never attended church. It seemed they'd rather drive the round trip twice—once to drop me off, once to pick me up—than to endure the experience. It's not that I didn't understand why they wouldn't want to go; the tedious sermons and lugubrious hymns were not my idea of a good time either. As for inspiration or transcendence, it never occurred to me to expect it there in the pews; no one had ever expressed to me that such a thing was possible.

But if my parents didn't have to go to church, why did I? You must, they said. Because. It was just one of those things, like holding a fork correctly, that were apparently decreed by some unknown authority.

Until one day I was told a truth. One cool Saturday morning my parents called out to me to come into the living room. They were sitting on our maroon velvet sofa, looking slightly tired.

"Sit down here," my father said cheerily, patting the seat of a beige rocker facing the sofa. Cautiously I lowered myself into the nubby fabric of the chair, slinging a leg over one upholstered arm in order to show I wasn't going to take whatever it was too seriously. My parents glanced at each other, but not briefly enough, then back at me.

My mother smiled an encouraging smile. She was indeed very pretty, I thought. Why can't I look like that? And then it came.

"We don't actually believe in Christianity," she said lightly, as though this was an amusing, insignificant piece of news from afar.

We don't?

Before I could begin to masticate this new information, let alone digest it, my parents explained further. They had never been religious, they told me, and nor had their families before them. After what they had experienced in The War—the dreadful things that they would later tell me—they felt that it was safest to be aligned with Christianity. Appearing as Christian, they added, seemed to be a good idea—at least in Australia, mostly white and Christian as it was in those fraught years after the war.

Apparently it was very, very dangerous to be what I was. The world was deeply hostile, so it was best to hide. Therefore I needed to pass, pass for something else, in order to survive. That's what I heard.

I also heard: Safety is paramount, more important than almost anything else. More important than truth, than self-expression, than authenticity. The indirect traumas of war branded me then through my parents, as it has branded so many others: each of us with a unique hue, indelible.

"Did you have to call me "Christine," I asked, the next day. " Isn't that going a bit far?" Overnight the news had fermented into an irritable upsetness.

"What do you mean?" my mother said, looking truly puzzled.

"Christine. Christ-ine. Christ-ian." My mother shook her head. "No, no," she said, "it's a nice name. It doesn't mean that." Sure.

But in any case, the fact that our family's Christianity was nothing but a kind of anti-corrosive lacquer certainly explained my parents' lack of church-enthusiasm. And it explained their unbending insistence that I attend the weekly sermons. The way they saw it, it was a way to make my life easier in this strange and frightening world.

Stuffy St. Martins had always been unalluring for me, but now it became unbearable. Being there was not only boring, it was now an emblem of deception and of my essential, terrifying vulnerability. If anyone here finds out what I really am, or what I am not, I'll be killed, is how I now felt, somewhat irrationally.

Any hope of a blossoming love for Christianity became remote. True, I was temporarily wedded to the religion, but I understood now that it was a forced, arranged marriage, a marriage of convenience to allow me a chance at safe passage. Whatever that meant.

I couldn't wait to break away, so that I could discover which God—if any—I would choose to woo if I were free.

Of course I didn't frame my dilemma in terms of a romance with the Deity when I was a child. But existential issues were, if not quite alarming, certainly demanding of acute attention. What *is* this world, and what do I have to do about it? What does it all mean and—even more important in an immediate sense—how does it work? Whatever the rules and laws were, they weren't particularly obvious, at least to me.

The annoying solidity of walls, for example. It seemed to me that, though I ordinarily couldn't walk through them, it was entirely reasonable that under certain conditions I should be able to move through anything. Why not, I'd ask my Sunday school teacher, Mr. Fox, for the purposes of embarrassing him. As expected, he'd blush slightly, shrug his shoulders and change the topic.

Time, too, was problematic. People acted as though time were just as fixed as a wall. Yet I noticed that it bunched and stretched like one of the pieces of elastic on which I depended to keep my underwear up. Wandering around my house, an only, lonely child, I wondered why there couldn't be people who were good at time travel or at least time manipulation. It was not until years later that I actually met magicians who juggled time in ways I was not yet ready to imagine.

But meanwhile, the questions themselves—what, why, and why not—were a beginning, as they are for everyone. Ten years later, half a world away, the questioning became far more urgent, far more real.

When I was fifteen, my father called another fraught family conference. Again I sat on the nubby chair, my parents on the velvet sofa, our apparently assigned configuration. This time I was alert, expectant of the left field lob. But this time it was a shift in home plate.

"We're moving to New York," my father announced happily. Wait, what? We're leaving soon, he added. He had always loved America: "The safest country in the world," he said, smiling wider than I had ever seen. And perhaps it was, back in 1963, just before Kennedy was assassinated.

I was quite pleased, excited to leave Australia. Though I had a pleasant posse of friends, there was no boyfriend, no possible broken-heartedness to imagine enduring. And New York!

Manhattan! Surely, I thought, there I could find meaning, excitement, meaningful excitement. Something good.

A word about the lack of boyfriend. I was a skinny, shy girl with no brothers to teach me about relating to boys. The all-girl private school I attended in a Sydney suburb never held dances or other social events. So, although I longed for a romantic relationship, meeting a candidate was maddeningly difficult. And even when I was introduced to boys, under the watchful eyes of my old-fashioned parents, I had no idea what to say, how to act. I was socially inept. In fact, I lacked eptness of many kinds.

America was a revelation, a crash course in reinvention, and a distraction of the most compelling kind. By the time I briefly dropped out of Cornell University five years after our move, the old existential questions had not so much been shelved as pocketed randomly. I never knew when I'd suddenly feel their touch: familiar and still inexplicable. And it wasn't just *why*, or *what*, or *how*. Now there was also, *what's real?* Yes, New York was exciting, the newly acquired boyfriends were intriguing, but still. Things didn't feel quite real. I didn't know quite what that that meant, but I was pretty sure I'd know real when I saw it.

Cornell wasn't real; neither was the Eisenhower-decent life my parents imagined for me; nor was any kind of pretend-worship, no matter how safely Christian it might be.

For months I'd been watching the TV newscasts late at night in the dilapidated lounge of my dorm. A youth movement—

as it was phrased—was focusing in San Francisco, the pundits said. Thousands of people my age were showing up there, looking quite uninterested in a navy-blue safety; instead, they were day-glow and uncontained. The newscasters were amused and dismissive.

But to me it seemed that something very alive, succulent, and significant was happening out on the West Coast and I didn't want to miss out. It looked more real, I thought, than academic life in dreary Ithaca, New York.

On my first California day I sat with a friend in a litter-strewn triangle of grass in the Haight-Ashbury section of San Francisco. The day so far had been a little disappointing; the streets and people seemed dingy and discomfited. But all that was about to change.

We leaned back gingerly between miniature hills of discarded cigarette butts, chatting with the five or so strangers sharing this struggling bit of greenery. Within moments a large flatbed truck, which had been moving very slowly down the street bordering the park, rather precipitously took a sharp right and bucked itself over the curb. Driving right up over the weeds and empty cans, it came to an abrupt stop right in front of us.

Okay. Whatever.

Six men spilled out the truck doors with intent and purpose. Jumping up on the flatbed they pulled tarps, clicked latches, unzipped cases. Within three minutes an impressive drum set and several large amps were facing us, attended by a thin Englishman with a pale, ovoid scrub of hair.

I wish I could remember now what he said into the mic before the next thing happened. But I wasn't paying attention. A black man, of no particular interest, had grabbed a quite interesting guitar and was taking a stance in the center of the flatbed.

And then a craziness of sound happened. A wild howl. The uninteresting black man had morphed into a guitar-copulating creature, creating music—or what?—unlike anything I'd ever heard before. Finishing, he lifted his guitar over his head, and crashed it, smashed it. He was a spider who destroys its mate after sex, or perhaps he was.... Actually, I couldn't think of anything analogous—the experience was that strange.

Within twelve minutes after it arrived, the truck drove away, the six men tucked back inside. The seven of us left transfigured in the tiny triangle of green turned to each other. Did you see what I saw? Who the hell was that?

A few weeks later, I saw the copulative creature on an album cover in a store. Jimi Hendrix, a name I hadn't heard before. That—apparently— was a Jimi.

And that's how California was—a Jimi experience—at least at first. I'd sought a rabbit hole, propelled myself down it, and found a wonderland way too easily. Truly, the adaptability of the human mind is impressive: after a week, everything that happened, no matter how odd, was quite within my new norm.

Nude people walking down the street, with pet mice crawling on their heads? Check.

Martial law, with police on every corner toting rifles? Check.

Waking early one morning in my bed to find a picnic, complete with checkered tablecloth, draped over my body, and unconcerned strangers pouring the coffee from their perches on the blankets? Check.

An epileptic stripper (she showed me her wigs and feathers) who donated all her earnings to the "revolution". Tear gas in the streets, night after night. Check, check.

If this was my new norm, you can see how deeply off-kilter my world had become. It was wonderfully, deliciously bizarre. Was I happy? No, but I felt I was breaking out of ordinary consensus-reality (I was wrong) while being fully entertained. And that was something. Wasn't it? It was amusing, it was risky, it was fun.

And then, abruptly, everything changed.

What happened was this. One morning, when I awoke, my purple and aqua bedroom did not look the same as it had the night before. Or rather, it appeared the same, but somehow without substance, flimsy. It looked pretty convincing—the way VR programs are realistic enough—but it was unnerving to feel that my world was one that was trying to pass for a real thing.

Blinking rapidly, I sat up, a little anxious. Nothing changed, the room did not solidify into the kind of of-courseness that I wanted from it. The familiar objects lay in their usual abandon on the floor—two pairs of sandals, a cup of juice—but they seemed drained of weight. Clearly unreal.

Coffee, I said to myself. Coffee. Surely that was all I needed. And English muffins with orange juice—the undemanding substance of normality, of middle-class ordinariness, that seemed suddenly most desirable.

Caffeine did not help. Nor did the immediate ceasing and desisting from marijuana use. Neither did the shower nor the bracing walk outside. A strange day, I thought. Tomorrow will be better. But the next day and the following days had that same strange quality. The world remained dreamlike. It seemed so obviously nothing but a thought. I didn't like it at all.

With a gradually growing panic I began to suspect that I was losing it. Either that, or the entire world was indeed a dream, composed of nothing but the workings of a mind.

But whose mind was it? Not mine, surely; I couldn't possibly come up with the extraordinary complexity, the punch-gut unexpectedness of the world.

Worst of all, I felt all alone in this insubstantial landscape that had become my life. I had no way of proving to myself that other people were really out there and were not just ephemeral players in what was rapidly beginning to feel like a nightmare.

It was only later that I read accounts of similar experiences in the mystical literature of Buddhism, Hinduism, and Christianity. In these traditions, the experience of the dreamlike quality of the world was usually a first step towards a joyful freedom—and to God/Truth/Reality/Spirit, whatever word is most acceptable.

According to the books, the happy version of this experience is usually completed by seeing that although the world is illusory in a certain sense, it's also very, very real—just not in the way we usually think it to be. The way it is real—so the texts explain—is that the world is not composed of separate objects but is, rather, one unbroken ocean of a Divine Intelligence. And nothing is realer than that.

Eastern religions love the ocean metaphor. They say that from a certain point of view, the events and objects in life appear —metaphorically speaking—as separate waves, even tsunamis, each one with its own shape and character and sometimes dastardly trajectory. But, from another point of view, they're all one thing. They're all just water, taking different forms. Divine Mind-stuff.

I didn't get the happy version of the experience, that time around, in my purple bedroom. At twenty I was totally unprepared and too scared.

Frightened and fragile, I packed up my belongings, left my aqua furnishings, and returned to Cornell and the upstate New York winter.

The Italian Guide

Two days after my return to Ithaca, my friend Joe and I wandered through the slushy sidewalks downtown, absent-mindedly kicking a piece of ice along with us as we talked.

"You see, Joe," I said, "I feel crazy. The world looks so unreal, kind of like a dream. And it's freaking me out. I want it to be solid. I want to be able to believe that the world's made out of matter, stuff. You know?" I pulled the scarf tighter around my (possibly) illusory ears.

"You're not crazy," he said, soothingly. Ah, so he thought my condition was delicate. He quickly changed the subject. "Hey, this place is new." He stood staring up at a sign above a curiously bare shop window. American Brahmin, it read, cryptically. With a sardonic grin, he put his hand to the door handle. "Let's check it out," he said, *sotto* voice, "how very Herman Hesse, how very Twilight Zone."

American Brahmin turned out to be a bookstore, but an unusual one. Instead of the usual bright display of books, there was a minimalist array of shelves dark with old leather and ancient paperbacks.

Randomly pulling one leather-bound volume from a shelf near the door, I carefully opened its smooth, indigo cover. On the fly leaf was inscribed, in spiky black writing, the name of its previous owner: Anthony Damiani.

As I read the name in the book, I immediately became aware that someone was staring at me; in fact, had been staring at me ever since I entered the store. And, unaccountably, I had no doubt that this as yet unseen person must be the Anthony Damiani of the spiky signature.

I did not turn; there was no hurry. For the first time in weeks I felt the possibility of safety. There was an inexplicable certainty that this Anthony was about to help me navigate the strange place my world had become.

He appeared to be in his mid-forties, though it was hard to see clearly into the shadowed rear doorway in which he stood. Thick, dark hair fell loosely above an unusually broad forehead. His rough, irregular features and the furrow between his brows were not inviting.

We looked at each other across the dusty silence. Immediately, a pleasant, fizzing sensation began in the center of my head. The lobes of my brain felt as though they were being pried apart, most gently, by a process of subtle carbonation. *Warm Coca Cola*, I thought. And then, *how ludicrous*. Each part of the thought moved with a strange, graceful slowness, like a horse in a slow-motion news clip.

How much time passed as I stood holding the indigo book, I could never recall. Somewhere, muffled and unimportant, Joe was using words, but they seemed oddly sucked dry of meaning.

The man suddenly turned toward him. The furrow deepened. "You damn kids think you know everything," he growled. Turning quickly, he disappeared into a back room. *Don't go*, I cried out silently to him, *don't go!* I had taken two steps toward the rear of the store before Joe grabbed my wrist. "Let's get out of here," he muttered.

Out in the snow, he released my arm and stopped to zip his coat. His hands were shaking. "What a weird guy," he said. Weird, most definitely. My thoughts still seemed to move glacially in my mind, cool and almost imperceptible. O yes, weird. But he will help me.

One week later I returned to American Brahmin, alone. As I walked in, the man, Anthony, was standing by the door as though expecting me.

The forehead furrow was still there, but now that I was closer I could see that it was a signifier of concentration rather than bad temper. He smiled, very slightly.

"Well," he said. "Would you like a cup of coffee?" Caw-fee. So, a Brooklyn transplant.

Sitting on an uncomfortable chair in the back of the store a few minutes later, I described to Anthony my disorienting feeling that the world was dreamlike. He asked me several pointed questions and, though I couldn't imagine what they were pointing at, I was reassured that he seemed to be following up on a possible abstruse diagnosis.

Then he fell silent. Leaning back against the slats of his chair, he closed his eyes. It was only then, when I was released from eye contact, that I realized that his gaze had a honed edge like a pick designed for a particular kind of probe, a tool of a science with which I was unfamiliar.

Again something fizzed and bubbled pleasantly in the center of my head. Delicious, I thought. Delicious, delicious, delicious....

Anthony abruptly stood up. Was it a minute later? Or fifteen?

Okay, he said, moving toward a tall bookshelf nearby. Sliding a book from between two large volumes, he handed it to me. The title, in blocky type on the spine, read *The Hidden Teaching Beyond Yoga* by a Paul Brunton. "Take this," he said. "Read it." Seeing my hesitation, he made it clear. "Bring it back. Soon."

And that's how he was. As I got to know him a little better it seemed to me that this unusual bookseller didn't really want to sell certain volumes on his shelves, that they were just there so that someone who might need to read a phrase or section in them could wander in one day and open them. Many of them were old and valuable—he had a 1804 version of Thomas Taylor's Plato— and were inscribed with Anthony's own inky notes all across the margins. Others were printed in India on cheap, prematurely yellowing paper.

Over the next several weeks Anthony gave me books to read that provided a conceptual framing of the experience of the dream-like nature of the world. Apparently mystics—Buddhists, Hindus, Sufis—often described experiencing the world as illusory, I read. In any case, whether or not it was ultimately an illusion, it was clear to me that it was impossible to prove that it existed as a material form outside our minds. Paul Brunton, using the facts of modern science, made this point in his books, and because Brunton was Anthony's teacher—he told me—I paid particular attention to his logic. And, of course, modern day physicists say the same thing.

Although the *apparent* unreality of the world was now not quite as frightening, I still didn't like it. It was unsettling, deeply. If all I could truly know of it was nothing but a mental construct, how was I to live?

And thus I made a choice that I've now come to regret: although I could see that the world was possibly illusory, I would ignore—in fact actively suppress—that knowledge. For the sake of my sanity (I thought), I needed to buy into consensus reality. Yes, I decided, I'm going to believe that the world is as fully material as most people see it.

In a way, my decision made no sense. Here I was looking for truth, while some part of me had its foot on the brake and was trying to shift into reverse. As *The Matrix* would frame it, I decided to choose the blue pill—that is, the dream.

After our first conversation, Anthony invited me to join one of the classes that he offered in the bookstore in the evenings. Every night, it seemed, there was a discussion group on a different world philosophy. Hinduism, and all its sub-schools. Likewise Buddhism. Platonism and Plotinus. Alchemy. Paul Brunton.

"Look," Anthony said to me —and it seemed to me he was deliberately accentuating his Brooklyn accent— "the people who thought through these philosophic systems were not stupid. They've got to all be pointing at the same truth." He figured if we could map out just how those systems were approaching that universal truth, and where the points of contact were, we could really understand things deeply. He was not talking about religion here, but philosophy at its most abstruse: epistemology; cosmology; ontology; metaphysics. I didn't even know what these words meant. It seemed insane. How could I do all that, plus finish up my degree at Cornell?

In any case, who was he and why should I trust him? What if he was just trying to sign up students so he could make money? It seemed necessary to ask him, but it somehow felt rude. One afternoon, using the return of one of his books as an excuse, I dropped by the store. Good, there were no customers.

Anthony was standing behind the counter by the cash register. He looked at me and raised his left eyebrow slightly. "Um..." I began, summoning as much mildness into voice as I could. "Um. How much do the classes cost?"

Nothing, he told me. Anthony apparently would refuse to take any payment or gifts for teaching.

And in fact, in the fifteen years that I knew Anthony, he never wavered from that position. It was astonishing. It was delightful. It was disarming.

A few days later I entered the bookstore to attend my first class—the one on Paul Brunton, just because it seemed the least intimidating.

Curious, I looked around. What did other existential sufferers look like? Surely only people suffering as much as I was, people as desperate to figure out what this world experience meant, would sign on to the kind of crazy study-and-meditate-all-the-time regime that Anthony was suggesting.

Two M.I.T.-pedigreed Cornell professors, one long-haired, the other balding, were introduced to me first. Then some fellow university students. Over time I met an ex-nun, a famous novelist, a Russian geologist, a tall man beatified by a halo painted on his motorcycle helmet. That first night, thirty or forty people were crowded into the small room.

Following their lead, I dragged a pillow from a pile in a corner, placed it against a wall, and sat down on it. One of the professors was fitting his legs into a full-lotus position, one foot folded up onto a plump thigh.

Anthony saved me from what would have been a painful attempt at imitation. Striding over, he adjusted my cushion, told me to just cross my legs, and focus on the words *Om Mani Padme Hum*, Om the Jewel in the Lotus. Much later I learned that this mantra is, in many ways, associated with the Dalai Lama.

But there I am, with my back to the wall. It kind of feels that way, too. Can I possibly plunge inward into a space that will introduce me to the Divine? That will initiate me into Truth?

The lights are turned off in the store, the street quiet and dark outside. The room too is utterly silent. I try to settle in. Om..Mani...Padme...Hum...Hum...Om...Mani...

I'm getting somewhere, I am. But then I hear the voices of two women chatting as they walk down the street outside. Trying to shut them out—and for God's sake not to eavesdrop—I ramp up the mantra in my mind. My tongue almost aches from wanting to actually vocalize. Om...Mani...

The women's footsteps have stopped, right outside the store. They're standing at the glass window, looking into the darkened room. Apparently there's enough street light so that they can see us sitting with semi-crossed legs and eyes closed.

"Look," one says. "Look at them. They're meditating." There's silence as they think about that for a moment.

"Yeah," the woman resumes. "They don't see nuttin', they don't think nuttin', they don't hear nuttin'."

The man sitting to my left gasps slightly, and snorts. And is someone across the room actually giggling?

"That's amazin'," says the other woman, her voice slightly muffled through the glass. And then their footsteps move down the street.

And—for some reason—that's when I know I will, I can, keep coming back to study with Anthony.

Anthony understood that I needed to learn to concentrate. Sure, I was capable enough in a conventional sense. I could write papers on sub-themes in Hamlet and apply the correct methodologies in calculus—though I had no idea what those formulations meant—but I couldn't control my mind.

I worked at the Om Mani Padme Hum, day after day. After a month, I'd come to know my mind as a kind of untrainable inner

Chihuahua. It yapped constantly, wouldn't walk to heel, and spewed unappealing contents at inappropriate times.

Anthony was patient. Okay, he said. Try this. Is there a holy person you admire? Jesus, perhaps? Buddha? Krishna? We have to try to get your feelings involved here. Think about it.

The next morning I woke with the words, "Lord Jesus Christ have mercy on me, a miserable sinner," revolving weightlessly within my mind. They spun beautifully, unimpeded, for half a minute before the rest of me caught on.

What! I sat up quickly. Where did that come from? Certainly not from fusty St. Martins. That church's flat, Anglican sensibility certainly didn't include this Catholic formulation.

"Lord Jesus Christ have mercy on me." And then I remembered: J.D. Salinger. After *Catcher in the Rye*, I'd read *Franny and Zoey;* this was the prayer Franny, the main character, repeats endlessly as she falls apart, slowly. Hmmm. In a way it was a little too close to home: the implications for the state of my mental health were unsettling. Though I was no longer so anxious, my fear of the persistent sense of the world being dreamlike still periodically attacked me, leaving me shaking, shaky, and wondering about my sanity.

No, no, Anthony rolled his eyes when I told him about the Jesus prayer, the next day. He almost groaned. Not that.

I was not to be deterred. "But you asked me to think about it, and this is what happened!" I protested vehemently. That something so Christian should show up seemed so unlikely—given my almost visceral dislike of my childhood church experience—that it felt almost like a supernatural visitation. It was too weird not to take seriously.

"All right, then. Use the prayer as a mantra. But don't do that second part! Miserable sinner—that's all you need..." and he walked away, muttering. Did I hear him say, "You already think you're a piece of shit...it won't help you"?

A moment later, he turned, and took two paces back towards me. "No, don't. I've got a better idea. Find a nice picture of Jesus—one that appeals, brings up feeling. Devotion, even." He suggested making a small altar—candles, flowers, if I liked—and then making my concentrative task a simple looking at the image.

It doesn't matter how you get yourself to concentrate, he explained. Devotion, even fascination, was useful if straight-up self-discipline didn't work. The point was to still the mind by, first, minimizing the contents, and then letting those contents drop away too. It didn't matter how one made it happen, exactly. That stillness, if one could get the Chihuahua to shut up, was said to be revelatory, a fullness. A step to towards the Holy.

Three months later I was getting frustrated. No matter how I persisted, I just couldn't quiet my mind. I wish I could report that the image of Jesus saved me. It would be so convenient for me, for the purposes of this story. But it just didn't work that way. It's true that my rickety little altar—constructed of cinder blocks and pine boards in a corner of my bedroom—was an object of reconciliation. Jesus is more than okay, I realized; it's Christianity, as practiced in most churches, that I don't like.

But still, it became apparent—in my meditation— that the question of whether to cook broccoli or green beans for dinner was often more alluring than my Jesus image. Or my Buddhist mantra. Or my tantra. Or following the progression of breath in my nostrils. Or any of the usual techniques for developing concentration that I tried successively.

Unreasonably, I felt both ashamed and resentful. Wasn't I doing the right things to attract Divine Attention? Didn't the Holy appreciate my discipline, my daily one-hour meditation practice, my new vegetarianism, my forgoing of worldly vanities in the form of nail polish and lipstick?

I'd thought these were the ways to please the Deity (yes, I still thought in those childish terms), but perhaps I was wrong. Perhaps there was another way. I didn't want much, I thought. Just a little something to show that I wasn't completely off the Holy's radar. That I had a chance.

Sick of my whining and my failures at concentration, Anthony pulled me aside one day before the meditation session that always preceded his classes. "I want you to stop trying to control your mind," he said. "Do this instead. You notice how the one thing that's always there, in every experience, is a knower?" I looked at him a little confused. This knower, or witness, he explained, is the observer of every thought—whether that thought was of bagels or quadratic equations or anxiety—that passes through the mind.

Now, instead of trying to control which things wafted through—the mantra or the holy image— I was to simply identify with the knower. Be it, be a witness. "Leave your thoughts alone. Whatever they want to be, let them be," he advised. "Just sink into being the one who knows them."

Settling back onto my meditation cushion, I looked around quickly. The professors were already sitting perfectly still, their eyes closed, one at either end of the room. They seemed not to be getting along so well these days. Across from me sat a man to whom I'd just been quickly introduced, a lovely man, stunningly beautiful in a square-jawed, Midwestern way. Jeff, wasn't it? Not my usual type though, I thought, and in any case, way out of my league. I closed my eyes.

The exercise Anthony had suggested was the second of the two main preliminary forms of meditation that almost all mystical traditions recommend. I'd failed concentration, the first of them. This second was usually known as inquiry, a looking inward towards that which was aware.

So there I was. Cute guy, I thought. And then, cool, I don't have to suppress this thought. Just observe it. Know that I'm having it. Wonder what he's like? No, no who's having this thought? And just like that, quite unexpectedly, the question of what was actually conscious within me became a tremendously interesting inquiry. I don't know why, it just was compelling. Within moments I'd forgotten the gorgeous square jaw. I was a tracker, looking for the source of knowing.

Is that the knower? No, couldn't be, because I'm knowing that knower. Well, what about that knower, the one behind it?

And then it happened: the thing I didn't know I was looking for, because one can never quite imagine it in advance.

The world, as I ordinarily conceived it, was in fact extraordinarily unreal, I suddenly knew, with more surety than anything I'd known before. Actually, it was far more unreal than I had suspected even in my most anxious times. It was a tissue paper illusion. Or rather, the worries and concerns about it were flimsy.

From the point of view I was now floating within, nothing could go wrong, in the deep sense. The real I, the one that I was, couldn't be touched by whatever disasters might happen to the body-mind coagulation that I'd always thought of as Christi. It was an experience of Ultimate Safety.

A huge laugh of delight and relief flooded through me, though I realized later that I'd made no sound.

Three weeks later I began to realize that something had happened, and that I should probably inform Anthony. I suppose that was the sign that I was losing the delightfully free state that turned out to be at the head of my personal river.

"Why didn't you tell me sooner?" he asked, cautiously, when I at last recounted what had been revealed to me.

Hmmm...well. "I don't know," I said. "I suppose because there was absolutely nothing to say." And truly there wasn't. It was the most ordinary extraordinary state. It was an Of Course state. As in, duh, this is how it always is, always was. Nothing to talk about here.

And yet it was the most freeing, real thing that had ever happened to me.

Delighted, Anthony punched me on the shoulder. That it hadn't occurred to me to talk about the experience—until I started pulling out of it after a few weeks—seemed to be the proof he was looking for that it had not been just a momentary delusion. "Almost a *kensho*," he said, referring to the Zen term for one of the first mystical breakthroughs. Then he reached forward again and clapped me on the back. "Well, now..." he muttered softly, and walked away.

Now I'd had a taste, I wanted it back. But it just wasn't that easy.

The Magician of Switzerland: Paul Brunton

Several months after that experience Anthony invited me to his house. We sat companionably in his study, nursing cups of weak coffee and munching raisin toast—a major component of his usual, dreadful diet—while his wife cooked a pungent dinner in the adjacent kitchen.

We were discussing my ongoing terrors. Though they had begun when I first saw the world as lacking reality, they had extended their reach, somehow, touching me when I least expected them. Something terrifying, something I couldn't discern, would leap upon me at any time—during a movie, when I was with friends, while I was trying on clothes in a store.

As I described to him the peculiarly extreme horror of these states, he shook his head slowly. "I'm not sure what it is, " he said, "if it's psychological or...or something else." He took a long gulp from his cup, and made a face. After a long silence he leaned forward. "I think," he said slowly, "that you should visit Paul Brunton."

My coffee slid perilously close to a sloppy escape from the tipped mug. It had never occurred to me that people like myself—regular women with perhaps unreasonable aspirations—could actually visit Paul Brunton. Anthony's teacher, I had been given to understand, was a man who very seriously guarded his privacy. And part of the reason was because readers of his widely sold spiritual books constantly asked for personal interviews, though he was quite explicit about not wanting students, devotees, followers, or anyone that wanted him to exhibit guru-like behaviors of any kind.

At this point he was in his seventies, trying to live an unnoticeable life in Montreux, Switzerland. The trouble was that, despite all his attempts, his obscurity was difficult to maintain.

It was the most peculiar thing. Sometimes (I had been told) when he walked down the street, strangers would stop him, an elderly British gentleman dressed in the unremarkable discreet attire of his generation. On more than one occasion these strangers would say they were stunned and surprised, but somehow had the feeling that he was an extraordinary spiritual being, and could they please, please be his students.

And not only that. Secretaries—hired to help him with his book projects— sometimes fell into mystical trance while transcribing his notes. It was inconvenient.

After I got to know him the stories were utterly believable. The man was a magician or a Magus of the most interesting kind. The kind that are in disguise. No flowing hair, no pointy hat, no wand. Those props are just for beginners.

But Paul Brunton (or PB, as he preferred to be called) had not always attempted to live such a reclusive life. As a young man, he had been one of the first Europeans to "discover" the Indian sage Ramana Maharishi, whom he then publicized in his 1934 bestseller *A Search in Secret India*.

Remarkably, Ramana Maharshi once said of PB: "He is one of my 'eyes.' My shakti is working through him. Follow him closely."

Once PB somehow received permission to spend a night alone in the King's Chamber of the Great Pyramid—it's hard to imagine anyone getting away with that now—writing later of a dramatic encounter with the powerful spirits that inhabit that ancient room.

But his real interest was re-presenting ancient mystical and philosophical doctrines in Western terms, using current Western science to help provide logical proofs for the divine nature of the universe. And he recommended that his readers follow an independent, flexible path to their own divinity. No slavishness. No obsessive adherence. No occult dabbling.

And yet there were many stories of his own occult powers—his ability to perform exorcisms that instantly freed people from heroin addiction, or to start broken cars by simply sitting in the back seat and concentrating. But in his books he warned of the dangers of becoming enamored of such powers, and counseled his readers to aim rather at waking up to their own highest self—the Overself, as he named it.

After he retired to his quiet life in the foothills of the Swiss Alps, he met the Dalai Lama who honored him as a rare and true spiritual brother. I don't know what happened at that meeting, but somehow some of the elixir concocted there helped set in motion the strange precipitation of the Dalai Lama into my house some years later.

But here we were in 1971, eight years before the Dalai Lama visit. Three weeks after our conversation, Anthony showed me a note from PB. In careful, shaky letters the mysterious author agreed to see me on a Saturday afternoon in a month's time.

Montreux, a well-mannered dachshund of a town, lies sleek on the foot of a mountain rising above Lake Geneva. After I arrived, I stood by the lake in the shade of a palm tree, gazing up at the slaps of snow on the peaks above me. Around me was a mysterious, tropical luxuriance of palm trees; carnival-hued flowers, which ought to have been described by words like *profusion* or *riot,* instead grew within the prim parameters of the Swiss love of order and control.

I spent the morning exploring the hilly streets, trying to outrun the jumpy excitement I felt about my afternoon meeting with PB. By two o'clock I sat, tired but still nervous, in a dim cafe, empty except for two elderly men engaged in a drunken yodeling contest. It had always seemed inconceivable that the self-hushed Swiss had once been a nation of yodelers, yet here was proof. Hiding my amusement behind a copious mug of cappuccino, I began to relax. A silky calm floated over me from nowhere apparent, in defiance of the alarmingly large dose of caffeine.

By the time I stood in front of PB's door a half hour later, I felt fizzily happy, although damp from the severe, hot climb to the apartment building in which he lived. This was a bland, aggressively functional new building of the type often seen in Europe, the kind whose architects seem to have tiredly succumbed to the convenient aesthetics of utility. It was completely unremarkable.

But the man who opened the door to me was more than remarkable. He was a small, almost petite man, with a trim van dyke beard. He was neatly dressed in a dark suit—the phrase *nattily attired* comes to mind—with a checkered bow tie.

I don't know what I had expected, but it wasn't quite this. Although I knew perfectly well that he had chosen to pass as an ordinary man, I suppose some romantic, childish fragment of my psyche must have expected the equivalent of a mane of hair and piercing eyes. I did not have time, as he ushered me politely into his apartment, to puzzle over why this demure man should seem quite so unusual.

PB sat me down on a somewhat uncomfortable sofa in his small living room. Large, ancient-looking scrolls and *thangkas* hung on each wall, and I briefly noticed several very finely-crafted Buddhist and Hindu statues on tables around the room.

And then he looked at me. I looked back. Silence.

"Did you ever raise tables, use a ouija board, anything like that?" he asked quietly. Why on earth was he asking me such a question? But in fact I had played extensively with a ouija board back in junior high school, and I told him so.

For those whose lives have not brought them into contact with such a thing, I should explain. A ouija board is a very simple mechanism designed to supposedly receive messages from discarnate spirits. It comprises cards, or simply scraps of paper, with the letters of the alphabet written on them, laid out in a circle. In the center is an upturned glass on which all participants lightly place a few fingers.

Someone asks a question; the glass then begins to glide quickly around the circle, spelling out an answer. Simple. And easy to derisively assume that the participants are directing the glass, consciously or not.

Although the glass had really seemed to be enlivened by some other spirit when I had experimented with it so long ago, I myself was never truly convinced that my friends weren't giving it just the slightest bit of help. We giggled. We were thirteen. We were just having fun.

"You, " PB said quietly, "are extremely mediumistic—you MUST get rid of that—and so you picked up a negative entity when you called one in for the ouija board."

What? Negative entity. Head-spinning, curse-vomiting. My data base, which consisted of one horror movie, immediately provided this thin, unpleasant dossier of images.

"Am I, am I possessed?" Was I really having this conversation?

"No, not possessed, but under attack." He smiled kindly. "This is the cause of the extreme fear you feel." I must have looked puzzled because he continued. My experience of the dreamlike nature of the world, the fact that it is composed of mind—he explained— was earned in a past life, through meditation and study. It was a good thing, but I felt some fear in connection with this—apparently it can take some time to get used to. The negative entity was hooking into the fear and magnifying it.

"But what can I do?" I almost whispered. This was a lot to absorb at once.

PB looked at me gravely. "I am not permitted to forcibly remove this entity, although I can help you," he said softly. "Though you will get help, this is something you must do for yourself."

I gazed at him, beseechingly. I can't! How?

"When fear arises, you must nip it in the bud," he said. His soft British voice repeated, "nip it in the bud."

I was not to give the entity the slightest thing on which to hook. Apparently, malign beings can only enter where there is some emotion or thought or obsession that corresponds in some way to their nature. Where there is no pre-existing fear or anger or addiction, PB explained, they cannot manufacture fear or anger or addiction.

And what about the mediumism? Why was that a problem? Well, PB explained, mediumism tends to go with ungroundedness in the body: the less one occupies one's own body's real estate, the more room there is for psychic squatters to move in. And—as I had found out—sometimes those squatters could be really, really bad guys.

He must have seen I was topping out on how much of this I could absorb, because somehow the conversation shifted to talk about my father. "He's unusual, and intuitive," PB commented. "You must help him to consciously get on the mystical quest."

He's already such an ethical person, I thought to myself. I swear, my mouth did not move.

PB turned quickly towards me, quite as though I'd spoken out loud. "But ethics is not enough," he said.

Wait, now he's reading my mind? Whoa. And that was just the beginning.

A difficult six months followed my return to Ithaca, in which I felt I was fighting for my sanity and possibly my life. Whenever I felt under attack—whether or not it was an entity or something in my own psyche, I could not know for sure—I nipped it in the bud in so far as nipping was possible. And when that failed I kept my body busy with physical activity. PB had suggested that I force myself to be more grounded in my body by moving it vigorously. Anything: jumping jacks, scouring the bathtub, scrubbing the oven. I had never before had such a clean house. And did not again until the Dalai Lama came visiting. Somehow this forcing of myself into my physicality did really seem to make me less permeable, less vulnerable. And we all know now that exercise is a medicine for psychic distress of all kinds.

One night, the entity came near me as I sat in an armchair reading—I had learned to recognize the chill of its approach. A peculiar coldness always preceded its arrival by a few moments.

This time I did not move, did not grab a mop to scrub the floor or attempt to wash a negligible spot near the ceiling. I was sick of the damn thing; it was time I learned to confront my torturer. It was going to be a showdown.

The cold thing wasted no time in its attack. It's a little hard to describe how it felt. I've known people who have panic attacks, but this was nothing like that. Imagine something horrific trying to seize your mind, something that somehow already has a tentacle-hold inside you.

I knew if it won, I would start screaming. How can I explain this without sounding quite clinically diagnosable? It certainly felt that what it wanted was my madness and preferably my death.

I ringed myself with a fortress of intention—get, away, from, me, get, away, from, me! The small hairs on my neck actually stood up, and a cold sweat oozed on my forehead. My will, its will. It tried to tell me I was already crazy, that fighting it was hopeless. Invoking everything holy, I pushed back against it. Fifteen minutes passed, second by second. And then, suddenly, the attack stopped. It was gone. I had won.

Slumping in my chair, I cried softly. There was no jubilation, nothing but an exhausted sadness. Please, God, may I never experience anything so bad again, ever. But of course I did. The attacks still came, but much less severely and with decreasing frequency. By the time I revisited PB with my friend Anna, two years later, they had become rare.

A few words, first, about Anna, though she deserves more. She was my closest friend in Anthony's group. Swedish, stalwart, and an astonishing force unto herself, she was a single mother with two small boys. When we met, the connection was immediate; she invited me to rent a spare room in her rambling apartment and I moved right in. These days she's well known in Sweden, as a journalist on a variety of spiritual topics, the instigator of a successful campaign to introduce stillness—a code word for meditation—and peace work into the school systems, and a main organizer of one of the Dalai Lama's visits to Stockholm. You can tell I'm proud of her, but it's more than that. If you'd known her then, you would never have imagined she could be such a player in the outer world. Back in those days she fell into deep mystical states so easily that I'd often have to shepherd her through stores with a sharp finger in the small of her back. Despite, or perhaps because of, the sharp finger, she remains my deep friend all these years later.

"How is your problem?" PB asked me. The three of us were sitting companionably on a bench in the sun, tossing peanuts to the swans edging the lake in Zurich.

But when I told him, with some satisfaction, that "my problem" was much better, PB said something that chilled me.

"You," he said softly, "will never entirely get rid of your mediumism."

I looked at him in horror. As always, he read my thoughts. He knew I was thinking that I would not survive if I had to continue to battle malign entities.

He smiled kindly. "There is," he said, looking at me drily, "such a thing as Divine Mediumism." What did he mean? But he'd already changed the topic, something about swans' preferences for Spanish peanuts. I supposed I would just have to wait to find out.

"You two should go to your hotel and take a nap," PB suggested to Anna and me after lunch a few days later. We nodded obediently and returned to our cramped hotel room, even though there was not the slightest chance of sleep. We were in our early twenties—hardly needed an afternoon nap—and I, at least, had an utterly inconvenient and annoying inability to fall asleep during the day under any circumstances, even submerged by fever or after a sleepless night.

There we are, sitting cross-legged on our twin beds for half an hour, telling stories, giggling. In the midst of an unworthy joke, I suddenly become aware of an overpowering pressure in the room, a pressure of bliss so strong that I know I cannot retain consciousness for more than a few seconds. As I sink onto the down comforter, I see Anna raise her arms as she too is falling back onto her pillow. "My God," she cries, "the room is full of angels!" Then all is gone, but just for a moment.

I become aware that I am in a no-space, no-time dimension. Everything that will happen, has happened, and is happening, is simultaneous. It's rather like a computer text file before you click on the icon to open it. At that point, nothing in the tale that's been typed into that file happens first or next; it's all equally there.

In that state, I understand that PB is placing a seed in my heart, a seed that contains my entire future development. Because all is all, without time, I see this future as one comprehensive now-ness, see which parts of me will flow to the forefront and what I will become. Everything that regular-Christi would love to know about her future development—and not just in this lifetime—is there.

And then, instantaneously, I slip back into the limitations of space/time. And find I cannot translate what I've seen into the stringent laws of my ordinary logical mind. That mind is habituated to time, habituated to space—and quite addicted to things unfolding in sequence.

How frustrating—I can't grasp a single detail of what I saw so completely in that timeless state; the software is apparently not compatible.

Raising my wrist slowly, I gaze at my watch. Fifteen minutes have passed. Although I have made no noise, Anna too is beginning to stir. I lie on my side, quietly, watching her. As she opens her eyes, she smiles. "All was one," she murmurs wonderingly, "rocked in a paradisical state...." This is how Anna talks.

When we ask PB, that night at dinner, about how he did whatever he did to us, he smiles and drops his eyes to study the menu, but not before straightening his bow tie. It's clear he is not going to talk about it.

Years later, I find the following in PB's *Notebooks:* "[the adept sees] the real, innermost state of the seeker, where he sees him [or her] united with the Overself. He persists in silently holding this thought and this picture, and he holds it with the dynamic intensity of which he only is capable."

And this: "The Adept's true perception of him [or her] is somewhere registered like a seed in the subconscious mind of the receptive person, and will in the course of time work its way up through the earth of the unconscious like a plant until it appears above ground in the conscious mind. If it is much slower in showing its effects, it is also much more effectual, much more lasting than the ordinary way of communicating thought or transmitting influence."

Apparently, I will have to live my life in order to find out, again, where all this is going.

A Good Man

Experiences like I had with PB don't fix anything, at least not immediately. They're useful as talismans to ward off the worst of the lonelinesses and depressions that beset almost any woman in her twenties.

At PB's suggestion, Anna had moved back to Sweden; it was clear to her that she had work to do there. I missed her daily, comfortable company.

The old place I'd shared with her felt even more dilapidated without Anna, but I wasn't home much. Cornell had turned out to be useful after all: I had an undemanding administrative job taking care, in some minuscule way, of faculty specializing in Asia. The work paid my bills and got me through my days. As for the nights, I spent most of them with Anthony's group, arguing Buddhist, Hindu, and Plotinian metaphysics until late into the night, and keeping my blood sugar from crashing by dining on crackers and string cheese.

This latter unwise dietary regime was Anthony's fault, but only if I'm in a mood to not take responsibility for my own bad choices. The way I can blame him, in retrospect, is to say that though he talked a good talk about the importance of balance, he exemplified it in almost no way that I could see. His attitude towards the needs of his body bordered on contempt. He himself lived on raisin toast and coffee, with perhaps a plate of pasta on Sundays. I'm not sure that I ever saw him eat an actual living vegetable, vegetarian though he was.

But it was more extreme than that. Apparently, the body was an enemy that should be given no mercy; giving in to its needs was a sign of weakness—and a sign that one wasn't deeply enough rooted in that which transcends the body.

You know what it feels like to have a tooth pulled without novocaine? Of course not. But Anthony did.

Once, when the repetitive waves of his diet had eaten away at enough of his dental frontage, he had to have several teeth pulled at one sitting. Great opportunity, he thought, to test his ability to go deep enough in meditation that he wouldn't be moved by the pain. No novocaine, he told the alarmed dentist. Just give me five minutes to prepare.

Four extractions later, he opened his eyes, sat up, and got out of the chair. It was an impressive performance, and it took me years to undo its message: the capacity to vacate the body is a good skill—and maybe it is. As a child I had actually practiced removing my consciousness from my body. Weird child that I was, I'd lie in the bath and run the hot water. I knew it would be painful—and indeed my skin would deeply redden. The whole point of the exercise for me was to remove my consciousness from my body. At a certain point I'd decide to reenter my body—knowing that once I did it would be painful and that I'd have to jump quickly out of the scalding water. Disengagement from the body, of course, was exactly what PB told me I had to overcome. And yet.

But I was happy enough, in Anthony's group, because it seemed to me that I was living a justifiable life. What could be higher, more *evolved*, than spending so many hours per day trying to understand the meaning of existence? I tried to explain this to my parents who, as I moved into my late twenties, were getting increasingly agitated by my lack of a husband. None of the boyfriends I'd picked up over the years had met their standards, but that was okay, as they hadn't met mine either.

Now that I was almost thirty, the situation was an emergency, as far as the folks were concerned. So when the news came that PB had decided to visit our group in Ithaca, they thought that perhaps the magician whom they had heard about could conjure a husband for me, if they asked nicely. They thought it was worth a shot. That's how desperate they were.

I did not know that they were planning this humiliating intervention. They had simply requested, via Anthony, via me, a little time with PB. And, like that, their names were added to a list. After they had their talk (*such a nice man, we felt so comfortable with him*) they didn't tell me what they had done.

Three months later I was engaged to Jeff, the square-jawed handsome man for whom I had so briefly lusted at meditation almost ten years earlier. The one who was out of my league. The one who had never shown the slightest bit of interest in me. Although I had known him all this time, our romance began within weeks of PB's visit.

Although I was astonished by his attraction to me, part of me knew that we were meant to be together. The knowing was deep and quiet and sure, even though my personality was merely beginning to learn what it was like to be with this man. And yet, there it was. A solid surety: marry this person.

It was only a year later that I found out about my parents'—and PB's—role in the mysterious and rapid blooming of our relationship. A friend, who was visiting PB in Montreux, mentioned to him the surprisingly quick marriage of Jeff and Christi. "Well," said PB to him, "what could I do… her parents begged me to find her a husband." When I confronted them, my parents admitted it. "But whatever happened, it's wonderful," my mother said. I couldn't really argue with her, as much as I wanted to. She adored Jeff, and so did I. Still do.

Sin

It was in my eleventh summer, in a dark house at a beach, that I did the evil thing. The one evil thing that I fear will come to me in the gateway of death and break me open.

Doesn't everyone have at least one of those? A bad act, a cruelty, a theft, a heedlessness? I'm not talking about drowning an ant, ignoring an aunt, stealing a candy bar, or bullying someone at school. Those are bad enough (I managed to avoid doing any of these), but I'm thinking of something worse, an act that leaves more than regret. It's regret wrapped around a nub of anxiety: will I have to pay for what I did, and how much? Will someone, at the pearly gates, sternly point me in a direction I'd rather not go? Will the laws of karma—you get what you dish out—impersonally and mechanically make sure that I suffer the pain that I've perpetrated?

Early that summer my mother packed some clothes, several bathing suits, a few books, a Scrabble game, dog food for my dog, Prince, and bird food for my green parakeet. It was turning out to be a typical Australian summer, the days and nights in the hundreds. In those days before air conditioning, the Pacific Ocean was the medicine for us as it was for most Australians; it was the salve, plentiful and icy along the coastline.

My father must have been feeling flush that year. He rented a house near a beach for a month in a dilapidated town incongruously called Avalon, the mysterious realm of King Arthur.

In the hot car we drove along parched roads lined with eucalyptus trees for hours, it seemed—my parents, myself, my dog, and the bird.

Prince was my companion, standard bearer, protector, and all-round good thing. I loved him as much as I was capable of loving.

But the bird was a difficult, unfriendly, anxiety-ridden creature. It seemed incapable of the most ordinary levels of companionship, not even the average pet-to-owner friendliness that's the pay-off for the daily cleaning of tiny eyeballs of poop staring up from the bottom of the cage, the daily filling of blue plastic water trays and scarlet food bowls.

I had owned this viridian creature for a year. Each day, resentfully, I would reach into the cage to do what must be done, pained that the bird experienced my small hand as a thing of terror that would send it flapping in anguish against the bars of the cage.

Until that summer.

At last my father pulled the car up under the limp eucalyptus trees that leaned against the beach house; they seemed too tired to release more than the faintest medicinal fragrance into the heat around them. But I was excited. I carried bundles of clothing into the creaky rooms, pressed my palms into the faded stripes of mattress ticking, and appraised a syncopated drip coming from the bathroom. The house had a freeing shabbiness, made delicious by my knowing that I wouldn't have to endure it too long.

I hung the birdcage from a convenient hook over a purple table in the kitchen. Afterwards I stood in the quiet kitchen, inhaling the strangeness of it.

And then it began, a rhythmic, skittering, metallic thumping above the garish table. I looked up to see the birdcage shuddering. The bird, it seemed, was jumping.

On the ripped paper covering his small floor, the green parakeet leaped up and down—insistently, persistently, crazily, willfully. It was an act most un-bird-like. Up and down he went, over and over, as though he had suddenly developed an enthusiasm for rigorous aerobics or been possessed by an alien force.

Tentatively I eased open the metal grate and slipped my hand inside the cage. Instead of fleeing it in terror, the bird leaped upon it and then sat perfectly still, looking at me expectantly, as though its wild tarantella in the cage had been an invocation for precisely this moment.

Puzzled, I eased my hand—bird and all—out of the cage and laid it carefully on the table. Why I would do something so unreasonable, considering our history, I don't know. It was a strange moment; the ordinary rules seemed suspended.

The creature sat quietly on my knuckles looking me in the eye. And then it suddenly unfolded its grassy wings and flew. Not away, but towards, straight for my face. This was the moment when fear could have flooded across the synapse from bird to human. And it might have, but there wasn't time.

At the last moment the bird twirled mid-air and landed skillfully on my collarbone. What was it doing? Slowly I lowered my head until I could see it. It was staring up at me. And then, abruptly, the parakeet tucked its head under my chin as though my bones and flesh were the cosiest of bird-pillows. I could feel its hot body relax against my neck. I stood there by the purple table, not daring to move.

Ten minutes later my mother came into the room carrying a teapot. She stared at me in puzzlement and then she saw the bird, its head still tucked under my chin. My mother and I gazed at each other silently as though we were witnessing an unspeakable mystery.

And so began a sudden and unexpected romance. This timid bird, who had previously found me terrifying now suddenly and inexplicably found me irresistible. It wanted to be on my shoulder or head or collarbone at all times. The whole thing was strange, perhaps a bit eerie. Nevertheless, I took to the intimacy—but selfishly, thoughtlessly, heedlessly. I didn't realize then that this bird was perhaps more than a bird.

In the mornings, I often opened the cage door and went back to my bed. The parakeet would fly through the quiet house and land on my head. Together we'd fall asleep, or I'd read and he would watch me, with the kind of love that was wonderfully undemanding.

Looking back, I don't know what got into me. Or what got out of me. Actually, it was neither in or out. I was in a willful semi-freeze. Looking back, I see that my parents' traumas had imprinted me with the feeling that this world was too dangerous a place into which to thaw indiscriminately.

This is what happened: I stopped feeding the bird. It wasn't a deliberate, malicious act. It was a simple laziness. I'll feed the bird right after I finish reading this chapter, I told myself. After dinner, I said. Tomorrow morning.

Tomorrow morning never came for my bird. But it came for me. In the morning, my bird was dead.

Ever since I have lived with a knowledge of my own capacity for a certain subset of evil—the omission rather than the commission kind. I ponder what circle of hell is reserved for my kind—those who let die, out of pure laziness, those who depend on and adore them.

Several decades passed before I was ready to confess the story of my bird to anyone. I told it to Anthony, who by now knew me well. Not well enough, I thought. I have to tell him.

He listened attentively. "The bird is you, of course," he said slowly. "The higher part of you. You made a choice." He didn't have to say more; I understood completely.

The bird was an emblem of the possibility of the descent of Divine Grace. This winged creature had announced an inexplicable, unearned love for me. Isn't that what they say about the Divine? It loves us unconditionally. We don't have to do anything to evoke that love. Except one day, we open some kind of cage door and let it come towards us.

And what a jerk I'd been. Far worse than a jerk.

If the bird was just a bird, I deserved punishment.

If the bird was emblematic at some level of my Higher Self, and I'd done what I'd done, then what? Didn't I deserve, richly, the withholding of the experience of the Holy? Oh yes, I was sure I did. But I couldn't help hoping that—despite everything—the Holy would forgive me and come flying toward me yet again.

God inexplicably forgives trespasses, I hear. I hope. Let it be.

The Spider Woman

Because of my experience of psychic attack, I had kept far away from psychics of any kind, something PB had suggested. He was concerned that it was too easy for me to pick up the dubious subtle company that hangs around some mediums.

But I'd always been curious about shamanism, the world-modulating practices of indigenous people of almost every culture. Shamanism doesn't seem to be about enlightenment—at least not directly. It's about tuning in to the fabric of our world so closely that the shaman can pull the threads, smooth wrinkles in the unfolding of events, or bunch up the past and future.

So when my friend Martha told me she had just returned from visiting a shaman in New Mexico, I couldn't wait to hear about it.

Martha was a skilled energy-worker herself, with a full client load, so if she thought that this woman was worth traveling to see, I wanted to know more.

On a cold September day we met for lunch at Cabbagetown Cafe, surely the prototype for all health food restaurants. It was the kind of place where the extreme use of garlic appeared to be more than culinary policy—it was a world view. But the food was, nevertheless, quite good and besides, Martha had suggested we eat there.

I looked at her, waiting, as two immense tofu burgers were placed in front of us. Martha was not a pretty woman, yet somehow, mysteriously, she was a beautiful one.

"What happened was this," she said. "I went to Santa Fe to spend time with Paola—that's her name. I've never done anything harder in my life, or anything more wonderful. She managed to push all my buttons, to make me confront myself." Martha paused, as though surveying her changed psychological landscape. "Something has really shifted," she said, picking up her fork. "Everything—the world, my personality, is almost unrecognizable." She said it so quietly that the phrase was denuded of its potential for melodrama.

"Say more. What's going on?"

"Well, what I feel is that Paola is moving me from being energy-based to being light-based," she said, shoving some recalcitrant sprouts back onto her fork.

"What's that mean?" I had no idea what she was talking about.

"Well, the old ways involved the moving of energy. You know, moving the *kundalini* energy up the spine, for example. But now I've just let the light in. I can actually feel it flowing in my veins. It's hard to explain. The experience of the light working is really different from that of energy."

What? I stared at her.

She went on. "Light is much quicker and it's everywhere. Energy is almost linear by comparison." She noticed me staring. "Okay? Are you eating?"

Dutifully I hefted a forkful of purple cabbage into my mouth.

"Martha," I said, leaning across the table. "Martha, that's...um. It's...um."

"I know," she said. "I know."

A month later I was on the phone to Paola, complaining that I felt stuck, spiritually. Although I'd had times of light and freedom, I simply couldn't sustain them. I wanted to learn how.

She was silent for a moment. "So when are you coming to visit me?" she asked. Before I could answer, she said dryly, "It'll be fun. I'll fry you, but gently."

Two weeks later, not knowing what to expect, and consequently mildly terrified, I hugged her in the Santa Fe airport. She was a brown, solid woman, with an enviable black braid flowing down her back.

"So what's this about being stuck?" she asked me as we drove in her beat-up truck from the airport toward her house.

I told her that for a few days every now and then I would feel a blissful power moving through me. And then, for months, I would feel nothing, completely cut off from the simple flow of the Divine Presence.

"What makes it change?" she asked.

"I don't know," I answered morosely. "It doesn't seem make any difference what I do or don't do. I can't control it at all."

"Oh, so you're the *victim*," she said, with the slightest tinge of sarcasm. For five minutes she was silent, concentrating on the flat, unpaved roadway, and then pulled the truck into a dusty driveway—hers, I presumed.

She made no move to open the truck door. "What's your practice?" she said, turning and looking at me with an exaggerated curiosity.

"Well," I began, "I try to meditate for thirty minutes on...."

"No," she interrupted. "I mean what is your practice?"

I stared at her and gestured helplessly. What was she getting at?

Enunciating slowly, as though I were remarkably slow, she said, "What is it that you are practicing *every moment*? What one practices, moment by moment, one gets good at, so you better be sure that you're practicing to get what you really want."

"Oh!" I was suddenly delighted. The whole concept of practice finally made deep sense. "Well," I began, getting into it. "hmm. I guess I mostly practice shutting out the world, protecting myself from experience...."

"Yes, you do," she said grinning at me. "And what are you going to do about it?" And without giving me time to answer, she opened the truck door and got out.

The next morning, Paola left me alone for a few hours. She had been called to do a healing on a sick horse owned by an elderly Native American man. As I was to discover, she had a facility for communicating with animals.

"Have a nice breakfast," she said, smiling at me as she closed the screen door behind her. Slowly I moved around her tiny house, showering, getting dressed, laying out rice cakes, avocado, and lettuce for my usual eclectic morning meal.

I was finally ready to eat. As I eased myself happily into the chair, I knocked a piece of lettuce to the floor. Bending down to pick it up, I saw two spiders sitting inches from my foot, their legs folded quietly under them. Their quiescence was only a small grace; their spideriness, and their alarming hairiness, sent me reeling back a few paces in mild terror. I have always been afraid of spiders; the spiders that inhabited my Australian childhood were deadly and hairy and aggressive. Fear of arachnids had been taught me along with my table manners.

Quickly I found two small plastic cups, which I dropped over the spiders. That way they couldn't come get me while I considered what to do with them. (I prefer sparing the lives of creatures when I can—too much needless death in the world.)

In Ithaca there are no seriously toxic spiders, but this was the South, and didn't they have poisonous insects down here? These spiders looked nothing like the benign types with which I was familiar.

I would have liked nothing better than to leave them there in their circumscribed plastic prisons and have Paola deal with them when she came home. But I didn't want her to think I was a neurotic wimp, one incapable of simply capturing a spider and putting it outside.

Carefully sliding a piece of paper under each cup and spider, I took my prisoners outside, and released them into the bushes, somewhat pleased with myself.

When Paola returned several hours later, I mentioned that I had put out two spiders. Her reaction was totally unexpected. Turning a steely face toward me, she icily told me that the spiders were her guests, that they had been born in the house, that in fact they were part of the ecology of the house in that they ate flies. They had as much right to be in her house as I did, she told me. All creatures, all people, had equal value for her. Was she serious? If not, she put on a good show; I apologized clumsily. Miss Manners, where are you? What do you say when you have just thrown your host's spiders out into the wilderness?

Later in the day Paola told me that she was praying constantly for the safety of her spiders, that they should find food and shelter from the storm that roiled ominously at the horizon. "They're baby tarantulas," she informed me, to confuse or clarify my feelings. How was I supposed to understand this? Was I supposed to see that though I might be justified in suspecting the spiders to be of a less than benign type, I should not try to control my environment so desperately?

Three days later, Paola sat under a tree in the tangle of foot-high grass that constituted her front yard and called inwardly to her spiders to come home. And damn, within fifteen minutes those two spiders came crawling up out of that huge wilderness and onto her leg.

As I have mentioned, Paola is known as a communicator with animals. She reported to me the following interaction: The spiders asked her if it was all right to move back into the house now. Although their experiences of the outside world were interesting, they had had enough. They told her (she claimed) that they were very aware of my terror of them, but they appreciated my gentleness in dealing with them. They forgave me, they said, for removing them from their home, and suggested that my fear of them was actually a fear of my own creativity.

It is an odd thing to be forgiven by a spider, not to mention be given psychological advice. But New Mexico is, after all, Native American country, where the respect for guidance from creatures is bred into the world view.

I'm only repeating what Paola told me of the conversation. Listening to the spiders' kindly concern for me, my natural skepticism flared and whined, but after all, those spiders did respond to her silent call. And when I saw, over the next few days, what else Paola was capable of, I was ready to believe almost anything of her.

Paola took me to the best of the tourist spots, graciously, without the patient resignation of one who has done this duty with visitor after visitor. She enthusiastically pointed out her favorite paintings in the museums, and the amazing apricot roses in a park. She was an attentive hostess, and she intermittently gave me hell. I remember sitting in her truck crying on several occasions, and on others, feeling so leavened with bliss that I felt I could probably propel myself quite well without her rusty vehicle. And she kept me entertained by revealing her powers slowly to me.

One day she drove me out to a historical site thirty miles from town. We spent several hours touring the ancient stones and a small museum. Suddenly, Paola looked at her watch. "We need to go," she said mildly, "I have to meet someone at the Juice Bar in downtown Santa Fe in fifteen minutes." She seemed unconcerned that it was clearly impossible to be back in fewer than forty minutes or so.

As we settled into her truck, she muttered very quietly, almost to herself, "Oh, well, I guess we'll have to time-warp." Exhausted and head-achy from the heat of the day, I barely paid attention. It was only later that I remembered that word, *time-warp*. Fifteen minutes later the truck pulled into a parking place conveniently vacant in front of the small restaurant.

"Made good time," I commented, as Paola locked the truck doors behind her. She glanced at me, smiled ironically, and turned away.

Weeks later, after my return to Ithaca, I was talking to Martha. "Did Paola time-warp with you?" she asked me.

"I think so," I said slowly, "but what is that anyway?"

"When she's late, she just warps time so she can get where she's going when she needs to be there. Beats me. But she did it several times when I was there."

"But *how?*" I asked.

Martha grinned at me. "I asked her that," she said, "and Paola simply murmured"--and here Martha gestured airily--"'Oh, it's easy. I just go into timelessness, move things around a little, and then come back out.' And I said, 'Gee, thanks, Paola, now I *really* know how to do it.'"

I laughed, but it scared me a little. Who *was* Paola? It was one thing to have shamanic powers such as the ability to converse with insects, but her capacity for smoothly and simply manipulating time was something quite other.

On my last day with Paola, she very obviously delayed taking me to the airport to catch my plane home. I'm someone who likes to arrive early at airports, hating the stress of potentially missing a flight. But perfectly aware of her game, I tried to suppress my froth of anxiety as the minutes passed; we smiled at each other with a transparently fake innocence, chatting over successive cups of tea. As she hugged me goodbye, after delivering me to the gate at the last possible minute, she said softly in my ear, "Things here are not always what they seem," and turned away before I could read the exact degree of irony in her wry smile.

Although she was extraordinary, I knew that her way was not my way, entertaining though it was. And it *was* truly interesting, but I knew I didn't want to focus my life on learning to talk to creatures. Or even manipulating time. Where would that get me?

Several weeks later Paola called to tell me that she was sending me some earrings. "They're beautiful," she said, "but I'm not going to tell you any more about them."

I eventually held the small white earring box in my hands. Slowly I lifted the lid. The laugh that rippled from my belly almost made me drop the gift. There, on the spongy cotton, lay two silver earrings in the shape of spiders.

They were truly hideous.

And the energy/light thing that Martha mentioned? That was yet to come—and from another source.

Mother Meera and the Glow of Spiritual Glitz

A new entanglement with otherworldly power began, deliciously enough, with lunch. Ordinarily I am a lunch minimalist, but on this day I'd been induced by an invitation from a well-known French composer named Alain, whom Jeff and I had met very briefly at a party a few days before. The promptness of his telephone call to suggest another meeting was surprising and flattering. I am deeply susceptible to flattery and moderately addicted to surprise, so it was with a hopeful anticipation that I sat down opposite his tall form, lounging elegantly at a rather unsteady wooden table in a local restaurant.

    Alain's mode was the erudite, witty banter that I supposed was required style at the gatherings of the Paris intelligentsia. He was outrageously good at it, but was saved from the usual brittleness of this kind of talk by a tenderness that I could not quite place.

We chatted companionably—I remember that Dante was mentioned, and the mad scenes in Bellini—while we ordered our meals and took each other's measure. Within minutes I knew I was outclassed: my limited, American erudition and balky wit had to work hard to keep up my end of the conversation. It was exhausting. After twenty minutes I needed desperately to switch the mode from banter to monologue.

"Alain," I said, picking up my glass of water, "I hear, through the inevitable grapevine, that you have a female spiritual teacher. Meera—did I get that name right?" A colleague who knew Alain had mentioned this to me recently.

He looked at me sharply, and then waved a fork as though dowsing for any signs of genuine interest on my part. He could smell that my question was mostly polite social bait. But the fork stopped. And then his long fingers placed it firmly, if haphazardly, back down on the wooden table.

"Well, yes," he said, as two aggressively healthy salads were placed in front of us. Two hours later, my gourmet vegetarian lunch still sat uneaten in front of me. Alain did not simply speak of Meera. And to say, rather, that he gave a bravura evangelical performance is also only partially accurate. Alain was not performing, though the effect was breathtaking. The calculated cleverness was gone. In its place was an astonishing spiritual passion, articulate and poetic and intelligent. Afterwards, I could not remember precisely what he had said, but I was left stunned and convinced.

He told me about Mother Meera, a young Indian woman who now lived quietly in Germany. She created, Alain said, dramatic spiritual miracle in the lives of those who received her blessing, her *darshan;* she had drawn him from an arid despair into an extraordinary world of continuing mystical experience. Lights. Ecstasies. Visions. The seductive paraphernalia of spiritual unfoldment.

Unaccountably—for I am a skeptical and cautious creature—I simply believed what he had to say. And there was something else. When he spoke, an unmistakable, luminous, ecstatic presence pressed voluptuously around us. This Meera, I thought, was surely the real thing, an unusually powerful spiritual being.

"So," he said, looking at me as he pushed his empty plate toward the middle of the table, "I'll be with Mother Meera in Germany this summer. You must come."

"I will," I answered, knowing that in fact I would.

Although I still revered and loved the Dalai Lama, I'd had a puzzling time trying to fit myself into the usual forms of Tibetan Buddhism; I'd practiced mantra, tantra, and deity yoga, and still I knew they weren't quite right for me—at least at that time. In a private meeting with His Holiness, I had laid bare my struggle.

On that occasion, His Holiness bent down to run a small matchbox car next to my small son, Benji, who was playing quietly at his feet. "Rmmm...rmmm," he said, and laughed. Then, he sat up straight and looked at me. Generous and open, as always, he encouraged me to follow the path that felt most natural for me. So, because none of the paths I'd tasted so far seemed "natural", it felt worthwhile to check out more spiritual methodologies and teachers.

Even so, it was absurd, really, to make a commitment to fly half-way around the world on the say-so of a man I barely knew. Yet my intuition told me—with a clear surety—that I had to see this woman, whomever or whatever she was.

[An Aside About Intuition]

Intuition, when it is working, is a magical, Mary Poppins kind of thing. It is the voice of a tender being, a personal nanny of the very best kind. This nanny is fixer-upper, a snatcher-from-disaster, an idea person when ideas are most needed. She convinces me to turn down the perfect job in a company about to fold. Sometimes she induces me to do whatever will make me decide, for however long, that it is worth incarnating on this planet after all.

Alluding to the intuitive sense as a nanny is a little cutesy, I know. Often I think of my intuition in other forms, but when the information the intuition delivers is protective or directive, "nanny" feels as accurate as anything.

Once she demanded that I apply for a full-time editing position that I didn't want—and knew that I would not take, no matter what. My life was such that I couldn't accept more than half-time work, preferably involving writing, not editing. Nevertheless, she persisted the way she always does, with her steely inner voice strongly advising me to follow her suggestions. So I sent in my resume and was scheduled for a grueling interview process involving several groups of people and three hours—a waste of time, I thought resentfully. Why put myself through such stress for a job I didn't want? But my intuition kept telling I must go. I was puzzled.

Two weeks after the interview, the employer called me, apologetic. I'm so sorry, she said, that I can't offer you the full-time position, but a new job has just become available. Would you be interested in half-time work as a writer instead? I took the job—it was exactly what I wanted.

Go to the Science Museum, Jeff's intuition said once, when we were in Toronto. Science, he said? Go NOW, she muttered urgently to him. So we went. As we got out of the cab in front of the building, a motorcade pulled up behind us. And the Dalai Lama emerged and somehow we were swept into his small entourage and whisked into a side door of the huge building and into a private tour of the collection with His Holiness. It was spectacular.

Another day, as I was contemplating cabbages, a voice clearly spoke in my right ear. "Pot," it said. I looked around quickly, but no one was near. It was a little unnerving. The voice seemed as real as if someone were standing quite inappropriately close to me. "Pot," it said again, more urgently. I had no idea what this could mean. Should I be smoking marijuana? Having given up the weed decades beforehand I was puzzled, until I suddenly remembered that I had left an herb stew simmering on my stove. Abandoning my grocery cart I ran out of the store, drove home cursing slow drivers all the way, and arrived at my house in time to avert a fire. As for the pot, it had melted extravagantly all over the stove top. The herbs were nowhere to be seen.

Afterwards I puzzled over what had happened. Clearly it was not just my memory of the stew belatedly kicking in; a memory would have done so in the usual fashion, with an image of the stew in my mind, and I wouldn't have puzzled over its meaning for a second. Nor did I think it was the Deity itself talking to me among the vegetables; rather, I suspected that it was something else that apparently had my best interests in mind. Perhaps a something lower down in the Holy hierarchy. Possibly a personal guide or an angel. Or intuition, if I was in a secular mood.

Of course, I'd read about guides, but had been a little skeptical. I'd checked out a few new agey books with hokey covers, scanning through them in bookstore aisles at various times. They asserted that each of us has at least one guide—with us for life—that tries to help us. These guides talk to us. They nudge us. In addition to our personal attendants, "angels" occasionally drop in as high-level consultants for specific issues. We may experience their efforts as hunches or inspirations or sudden urges to take a different route to work. And sometimes, when we're particularly obtuse, they may break through the usual Newtonian laws and physically move us or scold us about pots or use other attention-seeking behavior. Thus I had read.

By temperament I hate to be self-deluded. It seems particularly humiliating to buy in to scams, wish-fulfilling fantasies, and inflated ideas. But, damn, I would very much like the guide thing to be true. And I'm becoming more and more convinced that it is.

I know several people who, although apparently alone, felt themselves being shoved out of the way seconds before a careening object smashed into the place from which they were so forcibly and occultly removed. A few of these strange removals, some involving improbable hovering, had been witnessed by other people I knew. It's enough to make me cautiously set aside my innate skepticism and consider that otherworldly assistance might be a real phenomenon.

Of course, the existence of helpful spirits or angels has been noted in virtually every culture since ancient times. The Greek philosophers spoke of tutelary deities that are with us throughout our lifetimes and whose thankless task it is to keep us on track so that we fulfill the specific purposes of our lives. In the second century, Epictetus formulated the generally held view: "Zeus hath placed by the side of each, a man's own Guardian Spirit, who is charged to watch over him."

One Catholic schema—taken over by generations of cartoonists—places a good angel on each person's right shoulder and a bad angel or devil on the left. These are the personal attendants. And then there are the outsiders who drop in on special assignments. The Bible is full of these spectacular interveners: angels as lion-tamers, jail-breakers, demolition experts. They wrestle, they give advice, they announce.

Actually, the emphasis on angels is a slightly renegade viewpoint in Catholicism. The very early Catholic hierarchy became alarmed by what they perceived as an over-interest in angels, and in a consolidation of power formed a policy of exclusion: angels were no longer officially part of Catholicism. Some years later the Church reversed itself and cautiously welcomed angels back as a part of dogma. They've been there ever since.

The Tibetan traditions, both the Buddhist and the shamanic Bon, describe several layers of subtle beings. Each mountain and village has its own deity, as do each family and even the household stove. All of these deities are pegged to location rather than to individuals. If a girl leaves her family home in order to marry someone in the next village, she's no longer covered under her family's deity and needs a bridge policy in the form of a special spirit to watch over her until her new family's protectors take her in. At the next level up are a set of protector deities with which, through initiation and the performance of specific practices, people can develop useful relationships no matter where they may live.

Jewish mysticism lays out a complex angelography, as does Islam. Hinduism has its own version of subtle beings who can protect and guide us. Shamans from Siberia to the Amazon concur that such beings are real. My inner logician tells me that its reasonable to assume that the majority of the world's peoples cannot be utterly deluded: spirit guides—whatever they may be—may exist.

And if they do—if we are indeed attended by personal guides or impersonal angelic visitors or even our own higher intuition—how are we to know that the guidance we think we are receiving is the real thing? How are we to know if the hunch we're getting or the voice we're hearing is reliable?

I've learned the hard way that any bit of advice that comes with a flood of excitement is suspect. Apparent intuitions that came on like hyped-up, pushy salesmen— buy this stock right now!—have led, over and over again, to loss and dead-ends. Almost all the ancient wisdom on these things says that the hunches and voices that speak calmly are far more reliable. These are the ones that come as kind of inner knowing, solid and composed—or a voice in the ear, quiet and unnervingly matter-of-fact.

And that's how it was when Alain spoke of Meera. A solid, quiet knowledge that meeting this woman was what I was supposed to do next, cost and inconvenience be damned.

A few months after the lunch with Alain, holding my son Benji by the hand, I stepped out of the taxi into the wan German sunlight. Jeff was already carrying our old suitcases into the stolid small hotel that Alain had booked for us.

The Divine must have a sense of humor, I thought to myself, as I looked down the quiet, middle-class street. Does the Supreme Being stage spiritual dramas in such banal settings?

It is not that Thalheim, where Mother Meera then lived, was fully and unrepentantly stolid; as we observed from the taxi on our way to the hotel, the village was surrounded by an astonishingly lush and feminine landscape. Plump hills curved among tall pine forests, and the fields broke into meticulous and subtle blocks of color. But on this beautiful, ancient land crouched a charmless village of expensive concrete-block houses.

There were no homeless in Thalheim, no weeds in the yards, and no beautiful buildings; it was too correct to tolerate deviance. Unknowns and extremes of all kinds—grace and wildness and silence—should be crushed by such solidity, and yet Mother Meera had chosen this place over all others. Puzzled, I shrugged. "Come on, Benji," I said, turning toward the hotel. "What do you think?"

He looked up at me, grinning. "Adventure," he said, with all the assuredness of his four years, "that's what I think." I gazed at his coppery hair and golden coloring; with all maternal modesty I had always thought him a magical child. Perhaps he would turn out to be a prescient one as well.

That evening we found our way to Meera's ivy-covered house, wedged into a curve of buildings on a narrow street. A crowd of rather talkative people had already formed around the door. I looked at them curiously. I suppose I had expected the usual soft ashram devotees or sharp dharma hippies that cluster around holy people. But this was a kempt, conservatively dressed group—except for one young man with good legs and bad enough taste to wear the extraordinarily short shorts that showed them off to perfection. As I moved around in the crowd I heard German, French, Italian, but not a word of English.

After a few minutes, the door opened and the crowd surged rapidly into a hallway and up a flight of stairs, shucking shoes as it went. When Jeff and I finally emerged from the stairwell, the room at the top was filled with people—rustling, settling themselves cross-legged on cushions or into straight-backed chairs. A well-padded but plain chair against one wall was apparently where Mother Meera would sit.

"Jeff, Christi!" Alain was beckoning us from a row of seats draped with his magenta scarf. We barely had time to settle in next to him when bells began to strike the hour; the group stood up, silent and attentive. And then she stepped into the room.

She was small, drawn-in. Wrapped closely in a blue sari, she looked at no-one as she walked quickly to her large chair. A middle-aged Indian woman in a swath of pink silk bowed briefly to her and then knelt, her shining hair close to the guru's knees. Closing her eyes, Meera placed her hands on the woman's temples.

I stared at Meera, trawling for any signs of the extraordinary. The lashes of her downcast eyes lay heavy on high, round cheekbones that tapered to a small nose and chin. She reminded me of the delicate, heart-shaped face of a flower that I had seen once in an old illustration.

And then her hands drew back from the woman's temples, and her eyes opened. Flower, had I really thought flower? These were eyes unlike any I had ever seen, burning with a compassion so inhuman and fierce that it ignited the face around them into something beyond the earthly. Into something angelic—not in the sweetened Christian sense, but rather in the sense of the Old Testament. This was a face, I thought, that could have gazed forth from the burning bush itself.

Fascinated, I watched as the kneeling woman rose, and someone else took her place. What must it be like, I wondered, slightly afraid, to have those eyes stare deeply into one's own for the twenty seconds or so that she gave to each person? And what was going on here, anyway? Earlier that afternoon, we had spent a few hours with Alain. "Mother's way is through bliss," he had said, "not through suffering."

Alain knew he was offering a seductive morsel of spiritual bait. Who wouldn't choose ecstasy instead of pain? But I doubted that one could really go to the Divine simply by following bliss. After all, most spiritual paths, from Buddhism to Christianity, are predicated on the necessity and value of suffering. What else but indigestible pain would goad one forward, sever the attachment to the pleasures of this world? And even granting that Meera's path was a genuine one, was it suitable for me? Only one way to find out, I told myself, and resolutely stood up.

The soft carpet at her feet was matted, flattened by the knees of thousands of devotees. Kneeling on the well-worn spots, I curled around the suddenly erratic percussion of my heart. Gently she took my head and pulled it slightly toward her.

I don't know precisely what I was hoping for, but it didn't happen. All my years of spiritual training deserted me at that moment. Instead of the quiet receptivity that I knew would be appropriate, my human frailties and anxieties paraded through the self-conscious creature that crouched there on the carpet. Do I look like an idiot, am I doing this right, don't think anything obscene for god's sake! She released my temples. Surely she had seen what a ridiculous fool I was. Humiliated, I returned to my seat.

Later that evening, Alain walked us back to our hotel, listening to Jeff's quiet account of the great peace he had felt in Meera's presence. I was silent, letting the beauty of the vast field and the green light of the sky wash through and dilute my agitation. Too tactful, they asked me nothing.

The next night, Alain had again saved seats for us. "The hot seats," he whispered, as we sat down, "you're right in her line of vision."

Although I smiled as though in anticipation, I immediately dismissed what he had said. Nothing would happen, hot seat or not; I was clearly too obtuse to be pierced by a spiritual force, assuming that there really was one here.

Contracted by a sour hopelessness, I sat among the shuffling, sniffling, whispering crowd, waiting for Meera to arrive. It would be nice to be home, I thought, although the day had been pleasant enough. We had woken late, taken turns in negotiating the antique bathtub, and gone down to breakfast in the dark hotel dining room. At noon we had walked back across the buzzing field to meet Alain in his small room in Meera's house.

"Mother Meera's way," he had said, handing us cups of steaming, bitter tea, "is radically different because she works with a divine light that has not been active on Earth before." This milky light, he had explained, helps speed up the evolution of this planet and the beings on it.

Still pondering his words—ridiculous bullshit, I thought to myself—I stood up with the crowd in anticipation of Meera's arrival. And then she walked into the room.

One small, socked foot stepped through the doorway. And the world as I had known it was annihilated.

Instantaneously everything—the room, my shoes, Meera herself—was unmistakably composed of a golden light, pulsing and ever-moving. Impossible, I yelped pathetically to myself, I'm not even meditating! Astonished and slightly panicked, I blinked several times, expecting the golden hallucination to fade. But it did not.

Rather, the light intensified and deepened until it was almost beyond color, a brightness that disintegrated the individuality of everything within it. The chairs, the coughing German on my right, and I myself lost all contours and became nothing but a shining vibrancy.

I am someone who prides herself on having a logical, scientific mind. For an hour that night my inner scientist was silenced by the fierce bliss of the light, but only for an hour. And then it was time to experiment. Slowly I looked around the room. It was clear that the source of the golden-ness was Meera—she glowed so brightly that I could discern only the red *bindu* point painted between her eyes. If the light emanated from her, could anything I do affect it? My experimental protocol involved contemplating the most ordinary of things—the soggy, over-salted green beans I had forced myself to eat for dinner. No change; the light continued as before. Continuing the experiment, I quieted my mind by concentrating on my heart. And now the light deepened slightly, but the bliss grew so loud that I could barely stay conscious.

The abrupt rustling of the man in the next seat warned me that the meditation was about to end; somehow another hour must have passed. If I was going to submit to her outrageous gaze, it had to be now. Quickly I moved through the thick, glowing sea of the room.

This time I felt no embarrassment as I knelt before her. How could a creature made of golden light—with or without a scientific bent—be self-conscious? As she placed her hands on my temples, bolts of tawny light cracked from them and zig-zagged down my back; a miniature lightning storm played itself over the curve of my body. The gold light had been impressive, but this female-Jehovah act was beyond anything I could ever have imagined—it was my personal parting of the Red Sea, my over-the-top impossibility become possible.

Minutes later, as I stumbled in shock from the room, a man whispered in my ear as I passed. "Got quite a dose of the gold light tonight, didn't you," he said. I stared at him, suddenly afraid. He winked.

If others had seen it, I thought, then it must have really happened. It was not merely some kind of elaborate hallucination. It was not something I'd be able to talk myself out of later—an aberration of the psyche, explicable and entertaining. The light being "real" required something huge of me, and I did not know what.

Crossing the field to our hotel that night, I turned to Jeff. "How do I understand this?" I finally asked, with great emotion, "What do I do now?"

"Love her, of course," he said, "just love her."

It's not that I didn't love Meera or that I couldn't love Meera. I loved her, but cautiously. Over the years I got to know her very well because for some reason she took a liking to my family. This very private woman invited us to stay with her on numerous occasions. When she visited the U.S. she stayed in my home—sharing meals, washing dishes companionably—in between her public appearances. I fed her breakfast, made jam with her, took her to the mall.

Her power, unlike the Dalai Lama's, was of the glitzy-fabulous variety. She specialized in displays of light, in showing up repeatedly in the dreams of people ten years before they had even heard of her. For several years I functioned as Mother Meera Central for North America. Every day I received phone calls from people all over the world, almost all of them recounting one over-the-top story after another. An astonishing, couldn't-be-astatistical-anomaly number of them recounted waking in the middle of the night to a blast of light, centered around the image of the young Indian woman. Red light. White light. Visions. Ecstasies. There was no doubt about it, she could deliver. But what was it she was delivering?

PB warns, in his writings, that people should not be overly impressed with displays of lights—or clairvoyance for that matter. All the delicious and interesting ooh-aah stuff—just the stuff I found fascinating—is not an indicator of spirituality per se. It's a sideshow, and something that can arise naturally as one develops spiritually, but in itself it is not in any way an indicator of enlightenment. Rather, it's like a colorful foam that can arise as the pot of spiritual practice boils. Fluff, without actual nourishment.

A risk, he said, was that people could get fascinated with their own powers, were they to show up, and get side-tracked from the search for the Truth.

Not that this latter was my problem. But I really did want to understand more about what Meera was doing and whether that razzle-dazzle would, in the long term, help me towards my own realization of the Divine.

Both PB and Anthony had died by the time I met Meera, so I couldn't consult with them. And while I sometimes saw the Dalai Lama, I felt awkward to ask him to grade another teacher—particularly one who was not even a Buddhist.

One day, shortly after an article about Mother Meera appeared in a magazine, I received a panicky call from a middle-aged man. "I read the article before I went to bed," he told me, breathlessly, "and I didn't really believe it. So I said to Meera in my mind, 'If you're really a divine being, go ahead, prove it.'" There was a moment of silence. "I woke up in the middle of the night," he continued, "and...and there was a terrifying white light filling the room. It was so bright," he gulped, "I thought it was going to kill me."

This was entertaining, but I probably would have forgotten his story except that two hours later I received a call from a young man in another part of the country. "I read that article about Mother Meera yesterday," he said. "I was moved by it, so before I went to sleep, I asked her to give me a sign that she is really who I think she is." Now I was really interested. "Well," the man continued, "in the middle of the night I was awakened by this bright white light that filled the room. It was the most wonderful thing that ever happened to me!"

Some time later, I recounted these stories to a friend who was an old devotee of Meera. "That's interesting," he began. "Yes, I thought so," I interrupted. "No," he said, "what *I* mean is interesting is that the people I know who've had this experience saw *red* light."

"You mean this isn't unusual? You know people who've awakened in the night to her light? Lots of them?" I couldn't believe it. It turned out he knew quite a few.

What the precise significance is of dreams, or lights of whatever color, or ecstasies, or extreme visions, I don't know. But they're "spiritual" advertising of the most effective kind. You didn't know you want this—but now you know it exists, you gotta have it. Oh, yes.

Spoiled and Sulky

Humans sometimes want spiritual glitz—it's such a tantalizing glimpse of God-as-we-fantasize-him/her-to be. And we especially want glitz when we know that others are getting it. The habit of envy persists, alas. I had been thoroughly graced by PB, the Dalai Lama, and Meera, and yet—on a bad day—I could be plunged into a self-pitying sulk by a stranger's account of a six-hour bliss state triggered by reading a *Yoga Journal* article that I had written. Hey, I wrote it, so why aren't I currently in bliss, huh?

From a journal I kept at that time:

Lately I've been watching the ego thrash. It seems remarkably like a worm, bucking blindly in suddenly arid conditions. It is both ooky and horridly fascinating, all at once, and makes me want to look away, politely. Don't look, dear, a creature is writhing.

It goes on, it goes on, it goes on. It gets tedious. After a few minutes, how interesting is the twisting of a malcontented worm, no matter how articulate?

I seemed to carry my personal set of flies which I stuck compulsively in every ointment. And then complained. It was pathetic, and I knew it was pathetic. Habits die hard, I knew. And yet, and yet.

On days like this I would turn to one of my favorite possessions, a map of our galaxy, with an X in one tiny corner marking the spot where our planet Earth is located—if only our planet were big enough to show in the vastness of our local star cluster.

That X always put me in my place—when I remembered to look at it. It made me want to laugh with relief. It also made me ashamed.

Ordinarily my psyche filled the whole universe, crowding much of my personal Milky Way with spiraling cogitations and the same damn rotating psychological complexes. Almost all the space in my moment-by-moment universe was stuffed with great bloomings of my various smallnesses.

How could I fail to remember that we are all rotated and spiraled every moment of our journey, slowly and with unimaginable perfect speed? That map saved me then, and in the years afterward. Looking at it, I always thought that surely we are being spun and spun out into fine light. Though sometimes it feels like a black hole which, for all I know, is the same thing.

Meera: The broken engagement

Our tiny taxi pulled up with a yelp of the brakes in front of Meera's house. Yet another trip to Germany. "YES!" Jeff said, as the car pulled away down the narrow street. We laughed; it was a street-yes, entailing emphatic body-language. Benji and I looked at each other. "YES," we said, slapping each other's' hands, "YES!"

I must have been slow, turgid from the sleepless night on the plane, for it took me a full minute to notice the basket placed alone on a table in the small apartment Meera had built for guests. Carefully lined up in it sat three identical objects, candy bars apparently. The brand name lay in large, chocolate-colored letters across the parallel fronts of the shiny packages. YES, they read. YES. YES. YES.

YES Bars. Very funny.

"Could it possibly mean something sort of affirmative?" Jeff said. I kicked him. He grinned.

A photo of Ma, one that I had never seen before, sat in a frilly silver frame on the window ledge abutting the kitchen table. A tiny statue of Ganesh, the elephant-faced deity, stood guard near it like a cheerful bodyguard. A mysterious red powder had been sprinkled over his body.

I knew that these pieces had been placed by Meera's own hands. Moved, I looked tenderly at the almost surreal arrangement. What was she telling us? I had never seen anything quite so festively devotional from her before. Even her image in the photo showed her uncharacteristically arrayed in two extravagant necklaces and dangly earrings.

No powder, no offering, lay in front of her own photo. That was for me to provide or not, I supposed, in a form I was yet to discover.

I had never learned to be the devotee type, at least not in that cloying, fan-club, singing and hallelujah form that I have always found so uncomfortable. Certainly there had been deep love and respect towards all my teachers over the years, but no personal adulation. In fact, Anthony and PB had specifically discouraged any overt devotional gestures directed towards them. Whenever Anthony suspected that even the smallest pedestal was being slipped under him by a student, he would deliberately act uncouthly, or radically and hilariously mispronounce his words. Paul Brunton wouldn't permit his students to put his photo on their altars (we did it anyway), although his power was so great that he conveyed deep spiritual experiences effortlessly.

It was the power flowing through these teachers that I desired, that I fell in love with, that I wooed. I could love and appreciate, but not worship, the conduit.

I knew that spiritual teachers who accept devotion are supposed to be doing it as stand-ins for the Divine. Many people find it easier to direct their love to a concrete, human representation of holiness; they find the abstraction and utter non-abstraction of Reality to be cold, fierce, intimidating. But I was not one of them.

By temperament and training, I suspected that I was simply unfit for a full commitment to the devotional path, at least the standard version of it, which promised that absolute devotion to the guru could take a devotee to God. I could respect that path, even admire it, but it wasn't my way. Awkward, for someone so closely associated with Mother Meera, I always felt.

And now she had prepared this devotional display for us. Puzzled and slightly weepy, I stared at it. From his small pedestal, Ganesh seemed to give me a brazen, charming wink.

Before darshan, the gathering to receive Meera's blessing, I found Adilakshmi—Mother Meera's assistant—downstairs in the hallway.

Thanking her for her preparation of the apartment, I remarked how moved I was at the care with which every detail had been provided.

"Ah," she sighed, "Ma cares so much, she has so much love. She provides everything, everything." She looked at me lovingly, but sharply, to make sure I got it. "Even sometimes she may appear indifferent," she continued, "but no, she is always loving, and giving everything." Indifferent? What on earth did she mean?

Meera had always been so warm towards us. It would take me a while to find out.

That night, when Ma entered the room for darshan, I almost burst into tears. One of her devotees had told me she had just had gum surgery in the morning; an almost imperceptible swelling around her mouth reminded me sharply. She must have been in pain, yet she gave no indication, and promptly began darshan as usual. Dear Ma. For the first time that trip, I felt the old aching love for her, welling through me.

And, mysteriously, the energy in the room was more palpable than usual. It began to permeate each cell in the lower part of my body, strengthening it and opening it even further to the light.

Then slowly it rose, not up the spine as it often did, but through the core, directly into the heart. With the absurd extravagance of a peony unfolding, my heart bloomed one large petal of light after another, each more lavish than the last.

When at last my turn came to look in Mother's eyes, she held me there in front of her for a long time. It was not the usual light that I felt from her, but something that I could not quite discern, something fierce and so deep that I felt myself black out momentarily from its intensity.

That night I lay exhausted and wakeful in my bed, with Benji and Jeff snuffling softly on either side of me. The oscillations of energy within my body that had persisted after darshan would not allow sleep, this I knew. But what did I care? Whatever's going on in our relationship, Ma, I thank you, I thought. Thank you, thank you.

A few days later, as we were sitting down to lunch, David—one of Meera's close devotees—wandered into the group kitchen.

"You hungry?" I asked, gesturing toward the pots of vegetables and rice.

"I take just a little," he answered, flopping into a chair.

Years earlier he had told me about an experience of having the light pierce into his body. Here was my chance to ask him more.

"It was like an attack by light," he said. "I was in a panic—it felt like a heart attack."

"So what has it done for you?" I probed.

He rubbed his forehead, and grinned at me. "I have more sweetness, more love, more depth of feeling—oh God—such deep emotion. When I see suffering it is like my own. My sense of time is completely different, it's hard to explain. I don't experience time as one hour after another any more." He stabbed a bean with his fork. "But you have to pay a price. It's not easy. Everything is more intense because my being has become much more sensitive, including my body. I feel the weather shifting twenty-four hours ahead of time; I get sick if I spend much time with the wrong people."

The next night, I passed David just returning from work. "I need a darshan," he said, rolling his eyes.

"Rough day?" I asked.

"No. It was beautiful weather, pleasant....But," and he wrinkled his nose, "no joy," he said.

So darshan is a quick, reliable fix? "Does it always work?"

"Always." He paused, considering. With a slow smile he added, "I'm like a battery; it takes a little while to recharge, but once I'm recharged by her, I'm great!" He flexed his muscles self-mockingly. "Arnold Schwarzenegger," he said, "definitely."

Several of Ma's visitors had queried me, with some edge, about the stringent rules surrounding darshan—before, after, and during. Visitors were not permitted to hang around outside Ma's house; they were cross-examined, often unkindly, as to whether this was *really* their first time to darshan (if so, better seat). And then, in darshan, don't wiggle, move your elbow two inches to the left, sit here, sit there, don't do that. Once I watched a woman who had just flown in from America cruelly turned away from her reserved spot at darshan because Adilakshmi was convinced she had been there the week before; we knew she had not.

I had been brooding about this one day, sitting on the back porch. David must have been reading my mind, because he came over, sat down, and without preamble said the following:

"Visitors imagine that Mother is a delicate porcelain doll and that all us devotees around her have come up with these exaggerated rules to try to protect her. They see us as overzealous Germanic control-freaks. It's not true, of course. All the rules come from Mother, and she has her reasons for them." He stood up. "Of course, some of us overdo it," he said, smiling, and left.

Westerners, particularly Americans, do not take kindly to being ordered around, particularly without explanation. After David left, I remained in my chair, pondering the rules. I found myself still uncomfortable at what felt like over-control of the environment around Meera. I didn't think it really came from her, despite David's words. Rather, it seemed generated by a few of her closest assistants. Nevertheless, I noticed that a mother-rebellion was fermenting nicely within me.

The days became hotter and moister. By Sunday the temperature had reached the nineties; I knew that darshan that night would cleanse my pores if nothing else.

By the time Ma walked quietly into the room, the 150 waiting devotees were blotting slick sweat from their faces. Oh, God, I thought, concentration is going to be impossible. Indeed, distractions of all flavors were offered that night. A plastic chair snapped percussively under the weight of a large, embarrassed woman; several monstrous moths immolated themselves in the lamp by Mother's chair, sacrifices complete with odor, the sound of frying, and thin trails of smoke rising into the steamy air.

None of it mattered. Within the first few minutes, my back involuntarily began to straighten. This was familiar if rarely visited territory—the light of the kundalini surging up my spine, demanding and enforcing a specific alignment of my posture for its passage. The Hindus and Buddhists claim that the kundalini energy can bring enlightenment—or madness—as it moves through the body to the top of the head.

This time it moved from its home in the base of the spine up through my body in a businesslike fashion. No flowers of light, no entertaining imagery—experiences I'd had before. Only the bliss that seems to accompany the light wherever it goes remained.

The power swept quickly up to the crown of my head, pressing against a blockage I could not discern. What blockage could there be? The light seemed to move in and out of the top of my skull with each breath. Still, the pressure continued for half an hour, and then suddenly released. The light rapidly dropped down my spine like the mercury in a barometer before a storm. Ah, I thought, that's that. But it wasn't.

Now the light came at me from above rather than from below. A wide tube of light pressed down through my crown and slowly bored down into my neck and the collar bone. The process took about half an hour.

Then again the light flooded up from below, a final flushing before darshan ended.

Surely this was the work of a celestial plumber, routing out the constricted subtle passages of my spine. A skilled, delicate, and thorough celestial plumber. I bowed to her as she left the room.

I sat slumped in plastic chair in a hallway one midday, grateful for its muted coolness. The hot, heavy weather had continued, day after humid day. The house was quiet; I assumed that everyone must be out, working, shopping. But when I looked up, Raul stood in front of me, smiling his benign and quizzical smile. I had always been curious about Raul. He was a white-haired, vigorous man, perhaps in his sixties. It was his eyes that were intriguing—for as long as I had known him, they brimmed with a light and joy that seemed to be almost constant. I had wanted to ask him about it. Now was the time.

"I see white and gold light everywhere—from people, from the grass, from the chairs," he told me. "It's like a mist. One could almost touch it, eat it. For years it comes and goes; I cannot control it. Sometimes when I am busy working it is there; sometimes when I am being still."

"What's the corresponding internal feeling when it's there?" I asked. Raul frowned as he slowly translated this to himself. When he reached the meaning he grinned.

"Joy. Harmony. But also pain. Particularly when I touch someone. My body just hurts. You wonder why. It is because when the light is there, I am vibrating at a different level than most of those around me. My wife and I finally got separate beds for when we need them!" He smiled slowly at me. "The light is delicate, many things make it disappear. Touching people is one; another is thinking anything negative."

I was still thinking about the pain. "Did Meera suggest anything you can do so you don't feel pain?"

"The pain comes because I am not yet fully ready for this light," Raul said soberly. "My own vibration doesn't flow strongly enough outward to meet another's vibration. Instead, the other person's energy comes into me, and thus the pain. There is nothing one can do. I am a small tree; I will grow, but one cannot hurry the growth."

Still thinking about Raul's gold light, I wandered outside, hoping to find relief from the heat by the stream that flowed behind the house. To my surprise, Meera was sitting on a makeshift bench in her backyard. She had hardly been outside at all during the previous week. Several people from the house were sitting around her on the weedy, rocky soil. As I approached, they were having a vigorous discussion, mostly in German.

"No," Ma was saying as I sat down, "you cannot race to God. If you go to Frankfurt and rush through the streets, you will not see anything. Do not try to go to God this way, go slower, see the world on the way."

"But what about really pushing, meditating all day for a few weeks?" someone asked.

"People try this," Ma answered, "but after about three days they usually get a strong reaction in the other direction." She laughed, looking for a moment engagingly young and girlish and charming. She stood up, her thick braid swinging gently, and walked slowly back towards the house.

So. The message was clear. One cannot hurry growth, Raul had said. Patience. Oh, God, it was so hard to wait for joy and the knowing and the freedom.

It was July 4th. Late that night, after the last of the darshan visitors had left, we lit sparklers on the dark balcony of Ma's house. I held mine behind my head, showering myself in a halo of exuberant stars of light. "Do I look enlightened?" I joked childishly. That's how badly I wanted it.

Despite everything, it had become clear that Mother Meera wasn't going to magically liberate me, no matter how many scintillating experiences I had in her presence. Perhaps exalted experiences hack a trail through the jungle of the mind, show us the shining sea at its edge. But it's up to us to keep walking that trail or it grows over fast.

After years of being around some of the high-wattage spiritual teachers, I finally came to the conclusion, from surveying my inner landscape, that spiritual zaps apparently weren't enough to liberate me. I already knew it, yet somewhere within me there had been a persistent fragment of childish hope that a guru—if I just found the right one—would step in, wave a magic something or other, and make me feel all better. Permanently. But things just don't work that way.

Also, it was also time to face something I'd been relegating to the back shelves of my psyche for some time. Something I really didn't want to see.

Mother Meera. The problem was right there in the name: Mother. Adilakshmi repeatedly referred to the devotees as naughty children who just had to be reined in, fondly. It felt disrespectful and demeaning.

I was beginning to wonder if I didn't actually want a guru as a super-parent, the perfectly spiritual mom who would somehow save me. From bad things. From myself. From my ignorance.

Firstly, I didn't believe such saving by someone else was possible, though certainly one could receive help; and secondly, the rebellious child that I had been had already figured out the personal cost of such (promised) help: an infantilization and a willingness to override my own sense of inner trajectory. Were these feelings just the flailing of my ego, or was I actually hearing an alternate trajectory calling to me? I wasn't yet sure.

Adilakshmi came to visit me in our small apartment one morning. Lowering herself into a wooden chair in the kitchen, she smiled a low-wattage smile. "Mother has withdrawn from spending so much time with humans," she said. This meant—I assumed— that No, she will not see you Coxes privately. "It is not personal; you may ask the others in the house. She is not giving interviews to anyone." Nevertheless, I felt my tear ducts swelling efficiently; no matter what she said, this felt like a rejection.

"She has decided that it is better to keep a distance," she said, looking at me sharply.

This didn't quite make sense, and it hurt. "Christi, Christi," Adilakshmi murmured as I wept silently into her shoulder, "it's all right."

She was right. It was all right. After a few hours I stopped crying and adjusted to the need for a change in relationship to Ma. I had had seven years of unusually close access to a great being, and now that phase was over. How deeply over, I did not yet understand.

Sitting alone in our room after darshan that night, I was mildly startled by a loud cracking sound, followed by a low-key but persistent fizz of noise. I wondered if it could be coming from my computer, which lay on the floor among the conglomerate chaos that comes from living in a small space—in this case, some bottles of water, a vacuum cleaner, several pairs of drying socks.

Thank God my computer seemed to be all right, but what could the noise be? It was emanating, I noted when I looked closer, from a small pool of liquid oozing very softly from an apparently intact bottle of water. Puzzled, I touched the bottle. Instantly it revealed its fragmentation and fell into jagged pieces. Instantly I fended off the obvious symbolism. Hey, I was okay.

But it was strange that an unsealed bottle of ordinary, non-carbonated water should suddenly crack and fragment without any obvious provocation.

What was even odder was that a friend of mine, the well-known writer Georg Feuerstein, had told me of a similar experience with an exploding water jug that occurred when he was visiting Mother Meera a few years earlier.

Georg had been born in Germany after the war, and into a despair at his country's past. At seventeen he left his homeland, determined to leave all things German behind him. And he did. Over the years he became known as a scholar, authority, and brilliant writer on a prodigious variety of spiritual topics.

When he first heard of Mother Meera, he knew he must go to see her, even though this meant a dreaded return to the motherland. Being with Ma in darshan turned out to be a profound inner experience for Georg, but during the days he struggled with his revulsion and pain at being a German.

One day he was walking in Thalheim carrying a plastic bag with two bottles of water that he had purchased from the local store. As he turned towards his hotel, he saw coming towards him one of Meera's visitors that he had met the day before. This woman stopped Georg, and with some emotion recounted a visit she had just made to the remnants of one of Mengele's "clinics", in which had been performed cruel medical experiments on Jews during World War II. Her family was Jewish, and she had felt compelled to confront her fear of the German spirit. He in turn told her, painfully, his disgust at his country's past. As they stood talking, rain started pouring out of a sky that had been perfectly clear only minutes before, and simultaneously, the bag Georg was holding suddenly seemed to detonate.

Stunned, Georg looked down at his now-bleeding hand. One of the glass bottles had exploded.

The Jewish woman and Georg looked at each other, very damply. As Georg tells the story, the meaning of the event was immediately clear to both of them: The constricting, life-long agony that he had felt at being German had finally broken. "And it really is gone," he told me, still amazed, several months later.

Recalling Georg's story, I stood, holding the fragments of glass in my hand. Same symbol, but as yet no specificity of meaning. So, generalities: I would not be able to contain my emotions; my container was already fragmented and oozing; the merest touch and all my feelings would flow, and flow, and flow. Well, we would see, but I didn't want to deal with whatever was coming. Not if I could help it.

As we stood endlessly in line after line in the cavernous Frankfurt airport a few days later, Meera's airport darshan began. I felt this benediction almost every time I left Germany: the vibrancy of the atmosphere, the pressure in the heart. It was the most discreet of farewell gifts.

And it lasted, and widened. Two days later, at home, I still moved in that joy, in that certitude of the Divine's infusion in every moment of my experience. And my heart, miraculously, lay open.

Standing in front of Ma's photo one day, I thanked her. "Yes," I said out loud, "Yes, yes!"

But already I was aware that, parallel to the *yes*, was a surly *no*, roiling beneath the joy. It bobbed there, rough and abrasive, mysterious. And then it broke open, spilling and flowing all too familiarly.

The no was this: No, I wasn't willing, wasn't actually capable, of continuing to give over my autonomy, my decisions to anyone, even someone like Meera. For example, although she had specifically encouraged me to run my small publishing company (which published some of her books) as a business, she made strong suggestions that were simply wrong from a publishing standpoint. Jeff and I, as longtime directors of Snow Lion, knew what we were doing when it came to publishing.

The no that spoke inside me seemed quietly assured, as though it were acting on the authority of something deep and steady within. I knew, as much as one can ever know, that this was not merely the kvetching of a rebellious psyche resisting its appointment with discipline and self-abnegation.

My relationship with Meera would have to change, had already changed. This was scary, but it was only the beginning. I found I was angry—with myself— that I had tried for so long to bully myself into the submissive mold that was required in order to be in relationship to her. For years, it seemed, I had contained these feelings, bottling (how embarrassing that the trite is so accurate) them up.

Of course, I felt a melancholy regret. The path of devotion to someone with the extraordinary, beautiful voltage of Mother Meera was so alluring. And yet I couldn't take it—and still be true to myself. As Jeff helpfully pointed out, the *Bhagavad Gita* says that it is far better to follow your own path poorly than to successfully follow another's way. I was hoping that was true.

Taking from my shelf of most revered books Paul Brunton's *The Quest of the Overself,* I opened it at random. PB was where I always turned when in need—his intelligence, deep attainment, and utter sanity always came through for me. This time, as always, he was right on the mark.

"The true teacher," the paragraph began, "assists his disciples to find their own spiritual feet so that they can walk increasingly without leaning on him or anyone else. It is the duty of an honest disinterested spiritual guide to point out to his followers that their dependence on him is a weakness to be overcome, not a virtue to be cultivated."

Although I was ready to pull back slightly and slowly, that is not what happened. The break was severe, total, and sudden. It was bewildering and deeply painful. It took me a decade to see that it was perhaps necessary, as otherwise I may not have had the strength to really break free.

The precipitating piece was an action taken by Meera (or those around her) that put me in legal jeopardy.

It was puzzling. Meera had encouraged me to sign a contract with a British publisher giving it full European rights for one of her books. This meant that no other English edition was permitted to be published in Europe. She had seen the contract and given it her approval.

One day a comment in an email from one of her devotees mentioned a new edition of the book, an edition that Meera was planning to self-publish. Quickly I wrote to her explaining that she should not go ahead with her own edition, as it was illegal and could leave me open to lawsuits. Astonishingly she went ahead anyway. I was deeply upset, but still hoped that an open conversation would straighten things out. Things were bad enough, but then the situation became stranger. Meera claimed she never received my letter, but as she had responded already to other matters that were brought up only in that correspondence, I found that hard to believe.

Surely, surely this strangeness was somehow, someway explicable, fixable. This was not the first time something of this kind had happened. On one occasion Adilakshmi accused Jeff and me of something that was so completely untrue that we were baffled. A few days later, she apologized and admitted that she (and by implication, Meera) were wrong. Couldn't this be a similar mix-up? Suspecting that someone in her inner circle had been agitating against us (some were all too obviously resentful of our privileged position in her group), I offered to fly immediately to

Germany to discuss the issues. But she told me I should not. What the hell was going on?

For days I thought of nothing but the letter that I knew I must write to Meera. I needed to express my feelings openly. Tunneling up from sleep, phrases reconfigured themselves in my mind. Each day I would print out several newly modified versions of my letter. I modulated tone, even though I knew that her knowledge of English was not sophisticated enough to catch these minor adjustments of weight or warmth. Yet I had to be comfortable, in myself, that what I sent to her was as accurate as possible.

I concluded the letter with an affirmation of my love for her. I knew I was taking a risk, I told her, in writing so honestly to her. But surely any worthwhile relationship should be able to tolerate an open discussion.

One morning, after a week of obsession, I awoke, folded up the most recent version, and mailed it. It was enough. I felt calm and peace. It was done. What would be would be.

Meera did not answer my letter. Nor did she answer my fax a month later begging for a response.

Wounded and appalled, I knew that ethically I could not continue to be her publisher. In the dismantling of my small publishing company, I think that neither I nor she acted as open-handedly and forthrightly as we might have. I regret my part in that and have since tried to remedy my error, but have been rebuffed.

In any case, it was done. I felt relief at some level. Of course, I was saddened and puzzled and deeply disappointed by her actions and her refusal to engage in honest interchange, but I suspected that I had already gained what I could from the person-to-person, Christi-to-Meera aspect of our relationship. That was over. What was not over, I hoped, was our inner relationship. That was up to her. I knew that I would always welcome her extraordinary inner beneficence, as I had continued to welcome the inner blessings of all my teachers. Once or twice I thought I felt her familiar presence, the gentle effervescence of her light. Yet I was not sure that it was really her.

Then, one night, I had a dream. She stood before me: her silence was dynamic. From her flowed a force of light that pierced my throat, spinning the energy there into a fierce, severe luminescence. The next morning I wondered if I was being silenced or empowered to speak out.

We have not talked since.

Next

Several years had gone by since my break with Meera, difficult ones. I had been diagnosed with melanoma. My marriage had imploded and then improbably reassembled in a new, vastly improved configuration. A chronic, fluctuating illness that had periodically crippled me, one that had remained unnamed and undiagnosable for decades, received a name and the news of no reasonable cure. And so on.

Lying in my house with months of significant fever, I sometimes felt like an almost inert substance, one that required the presence of other humans to come alive. Someone would visit—a reagent—and I'd begin to fizz with ideas and conversation and kindness. Afterwards I'd sink back into dormancy.

It had been a strange time. There were some weeks of happiness, weeks of despair, all of them seemingly directed, produced, and cast by capricious biochemicals. Cortisol. Serotonin. Dopamine. Norepinephrine. They were forces of nature; I knew enough not to take their disaster-flick scenarios too seriously, but still.

With luck and grace, I would occasionally remember to pray through the storm. Or the drought. My map of the universe helped relativize things, but only briefly. Now I'd reached the point where desperation transmutes to fervency. Fervency came upon me like a purifying fever. It took the form of prayer.

And this is what I prayed for: fullness, passion, connection. The plug meeting its socket and the appliance coming to life. Any damn kind of forward momentum, please. And sure enough, something showed up, a zig when I thought I wanted zag.

The gods are mysterious. They joke around a lot, but keep their eyes on the ball, or balls, flying every which way in perfect time to the rhythm of unfoldment. They take their time—it belongs to them in any case. But then, perfect jugglers that they are, it seems that they allow the perfect object to land right in your hand when you least expect it.

Speaking Up and Out

"You like to think of yourself as an unusually sensitive, warm male," I say to the leader of a weekend seminar, "but you just come off as conceited and manipulative." Fifty people in the group are looking at me; I imagine that they are appalled, that they will reject me forever for speaking out this way. But I know I have to do it.

I am ordinarily a quiet-ish person, shy and polite. Ordinarily I would never say such a thing, especially in front of a group. But this is my third weekend in a multi-year-long program that encourages a let-it-hang-out honesty—and I figure I might as well begin with the teacher. If he can't take it, who can?

And truly, I'm a little thrilled to be given permission to act out. I get to experiment with being a different kind of social creature—a troublemaker. I go against the social grain in various small ways. It feels good. It feels risky. It feels necessary.

I open my mouth, but bigger than usual. I open my mouth all the way down to my throat. All the better to speak the truth, m'dear. Heh heh heh.

I began opening my mouth young. Every baby photo shows the joyous gape in the center of my face. Not just a crescent of mouth but the full moon howl of ecstasy.

But by the time I turned seven my mouth was closed, according to the gray images mounted on stale paper in an old photo album. I'd figured out that a mouth is a dangerous thing to open. More dangerous than any other orifice. Just as dangerous as what comes in is what comes out. You can spend years crafting things—relationships, a persona, safety—and one day when the throat is relaxed, the gut shoots a verbal BB right up the esophagus, out between the teeth, into the face of your dad or your best friend, Margaret, who never talks to you again.

So, here I am, decades later. I have experimentally allowed my BB to propel towards the one authority in the room—the seminar leader, He Who Knows. It's a pivotal moment in our relationship.

He Who Knows looks me, and then speaks to me as does a sensitive, warm male. He is reliably manipulative, but I see that I've passed some kind of test. He has too.

He, and this workshop, are funneling life and motion into me just when I needed it most.

Through several years of weekend workshops, he infuriated me, and he taught me a lot. Mostly, he encouraged me to speak up and out, no matter the cost. I'd already started, of course. My Mother Meera experience had tested me, I think, to see if I could/would say what needed to be said when something came hard against my sense of ethics.

HWK took me further: expressing myself openly as an everyday way of life. Of course, I initially got it wrong. I spoke out when it was neither kind nor necessary. (Necessary is the operative word, the one I've tried to install as a filter somewhere below my voice box. It slips. It goes missing. It's sometimes overcome by stronger words and wimps out. And then, when I most hope for it to block something I'm afraid to say, it inconveniently steps aside to let me know that yes, it's necessary that I say the scary thing, the thing with possible scary consequences.)

My intuition kept insisting that developing the habit of honest communication was a key part of my spiritual development. Why the emphasis came now, at this particular point of my trajectory, I didn't know—and it was a little surprising. But there it was.

Of course, my commitment to speaking out brought up the question of deception: when it might be a good thing, and when it fast-tracks you to whatever hell fits your belief system.

In my parents' world view, lying was a necessary thing. My parents were not of the school that dies for truth; they were of the school that lies for life. They knew that if you lie well enough, you could pass yourself off as something other than what you were, something that might keep you alive.

In my childhood, their stories emerged, each one astonishing enough, even though I'm sure they must have been edited down to PG. In all of them the saving, heroic gesture was always a successful deception.

Some examples: Desperate to flee a small town in Hungary, in which a thorough investigation of identity papers was being waged, my mother—who was barely passing as a governess for a wealthy family—finagled a ride to a safer town with a top Nazi official. I imagine her there, in the back of the chauffeured vehicle, an exceptionally attractive, dark-haired girl with the prettiest up-turned nose. The officer flirts, I know that much. My mother only alluded to the full price she paid for this necessary ride. Her lifelong depression and anxiety gave an indication of the cost. But she stayed alive.

My vain grandparents stranded their hair with precious flour and smeared their upper-class faces with soot so that they could pass for old people when the Nazis rounded up everyone under fifty and shipped them off to work camps.

My aunt, acting as an oddly benevolent stranger, bought her husband's freedom from a prison with a diamond ring. "I don't know him, but I've heard good things about his family," she told the Nazi official as she handed over the ring.

The unspoken message: Deception, well chosen, is to be celebrated. At the same time, the spoken message: Don't ever lie.

[an aside about lies]

Doesn't everybody engage in deceptions of some kind or another? The average human tells a lie at least twenty-five times a day, according to a scientist at the University of Massachusetts. Astonishing. I'm fairly sure that I don't lie that frequently and neither do my friends—or so I hope. But if we're not putting in our twenty-five, there must be a lot of overactive liars out there, wagging their forked tongues hundreds of times a day and torquing the statistics.

It's not that I don't lie. Probably every week I say at least one of these:

> Everything's fine.
>
> No, really, I don't mind.
>
> Mmm, delicious.
>
> I'd love to.

White lies. Relatively harmless deceptions, I used to think. But many spiritual traditions seem to have a different view. "Lying lips are abomination to the Lord," pontificates Proverbs 12. Apparently telling a lie is abominable. I never quite understood it. Why aren't white lies, at least, a good thing? They save incalculable amounts of hurt feelings about small, unimportant things. What could be wrong with that?

This is what's wrong with it, according to some Buddhist texts: Hiding the truth apparently damages the subtle organ for *recognizing* the truth. It seems sort-of fair; if you deny someone the truth you too will be denied the truth. This becomes acutely important when we're talking about the truth that really counts, the big one: the Real, the Holy, the Ultimately Authentic.

At a convivial dinner some time back, I engaged eight of my friends—all of them active practitioners of various spiritual traditions—in a discussion about lying. All of them confessed, when I put them on the spot, that they told white lies. In revenge one gazed winningly into my eyes and whispered that my rice was simply the most delicious rice he had ever eaten; the napkin I threw missed him by a few inches, but still.

It seems that we who like to think of ourselves as spiritual people routinely indulge in pale deceptions. I wondered how we could justify it to ourselves, given how serious we were about not killing, stealing, and perpetrating other hurtful acts.

One woman pointed out that the Dalai Lama speaks about the kind of lies my parents valued. Although he makes it clear that ordinarily we should not lie, he also says that there can be "occasions involving the safety and welfare of other people when we can sometimes tell a lie," which seems eminently reasonable.

The Bible's stance is somewhat equivocal. Although the Proverb quoted earlier is utterly unambiguous and Jesus clearly says "Do not tell lies" (Matthew 19), lying does not appear in the Ten Commandments—a peculiarity. The closest the commandments get is to ask us not to bear false witness against a neighbor, but nothing about not convincing her that her new haircut isn't all that bad. Neither is lying one of the Seven Deadly Sins, which are defined as those things that block spiritual progress.

All of this adds up to historically ambiguous attitudes toward shading the truth. Judging from the religious texts, it's not a top-of-the list moral failing. It's a mid-range act that can veer toward virtue or sin depending upon its motivation. The operative issue seems to be whether or not the lie benefits the perpetrator in any way. For example, denying adultery–even though it may protect the delicate feelings of the spouse—is moved primarily by a self-serving, save-my-ass impulse. The fact that there's a bit of compassion mixed in does not make it a virtue.

Though I wasn't ready to commit to total pure-as-the-driven-snow truthfulness at every moment, I couldn't avoid the conclusion that life was pushing me towards a commitment to speaking up and out as needed, no matter the consequences.

With He Who Knows I slowly learned to modulate my experimental attack-dog version of honesty so that it became more appropriate for life outside the weekend play-group. It became clear to me that my edges—when I let them show—could be too sharp. That when I only mean to pry something apart a little with a bit of sharp logic, I could draw blood. Surely it's better to be a spoon than a knife, I thought, better to be an (honest) implement of tenderness. It was tricky.

Adyashanti, a beloved spiritual teacher whom I later met, invites students to try an experiment of speaking truthfully for twenty-four hours: no white lies, no sugar-coating. Since he considers enlightenment to be the crumbling away of untruth, speaking only what's true is an important step. Knowing him, I'm sure he means an honesty gently tempered.

I must add this: He Who Knows was Levent Bolukbasi, a passionate Turk. He was a wonderful human being.

Be Here Now vs Be Bliss Sometime

At some point during this time, I gradually became aware of myself as an ocean of light, a vast sea connected to this world by a narrow and defective faucet—my pathetic ego. Until that faucet loosened, so little could flow through it to the level on which I was living my life that I would forget the vastness that fed the erratic trickle. But now—for no reason that I could discern—the light streamed through me with such force that my cramped ego felt it would burst. Perhaps it had to do with my increased truth-telling.

I noticed that the brightness intensified when I was talking to someone, as though the light itself wanted to communicate with whomever I was with. It would begin as a a heat that quickly fanned into a conflagration in my heart. Although I call it heat, it was equally love, and sometimes I almost fainted from its intensity. I could feel this heat/love pour out of my chest towards the person, who was usually unaware of my pyromania. Sometimes the light would direct my words—a few sentences usually—that would turn out to be important to the person in some way. As I observed myself delivering what felt like divine mail, I remembered PB: There is such a thing as divine mediumism. Was this what he meant? Perhaps it was not something to fear after all. And perhaps learning to speak up, no matter what, was not just about my own personal well-being.

At first these events were unusual, and left me elated but exhausted. But gradually I learned to hold the energy for longer periods and it became a constant in my life.

Those months were blissful, undisturbed by the anxieties I ordinarily lived with. After all, it was clear that the Divine was in control, was running the show. Everything that happened seemed therefore perfect, however unpleasant it might look to the ego. My life had become a meditation on the constant ecstasy of the ordinary.

Self-doubter that I am, I wondered if I were deluded or inflated—joyfully suffering from some variety of religious psychosis. But my friends reassured me that I seemed fairly sane.

Just as I was beginning to think this state was mine, the aperture to the light narrowed. And kept narrowing. At first I was indignant—and then I felt chastened. Too much ego in me, of course. The whole thing had been merely on loan to me—from the Great Wherever. I didn't earn it, hadn't paid the unknown price, and apparently couldn't keep it. The endless lesson of my life: "spiritual" experiences come and go, damn it, just like everything else in life. Get over it, I kept telling myself.

Though it had been delightful, I knew the state was not an enlightened one. It was not an awakened, liberated condition, which is not a state at all, but a conscious stepping fully into that which we all are already in our fullness. Perhaps the delicious love/heat had disappeared to force me to do the real work, the stepping back from identification with the ego, with its tedious eagerness to feel expanded and virtuous and glowy—and with its anxious tentacles spreading into past and future.

And so I turned to trying to focus on the present moment. On being less seduced by the past and the future, not robbing the cradle before it had even been filled with the coming, unborn moment. Nor wallowing around (too much) with the past, which is, after all, always beyond its prime, and not altogether hygienic. I aimed for no more seduction, no more enamorment with anything but the current burst of experience, which, as we have been told, is really where it's at. Be here now.

Slowly I was learning to be on the prow of my life, rather than hiding somewhere in the hull. This meant going forth heart first, entering my world less tentatively. It was not comfortable. The me that had a tendency toward mediumism—the one who wasn't firmly rooted in her body—still found the world frightening. Life in the body, with trauma and pain possible at any moment, seemed far too dangerous. That me preferred to withdraw into her thoughts, to read her books.

I had never loved life enough—it seemed to me. I knew that my lack of appreciation was rude to the Divine, who after all provides this entertainment. It's the Holy's movie, I thought, and the least I could do was applaud the nice use of color and ingenious application of special effects even if the story line often was disturbing. I could (theoretically) learn to appreciate every minute, just as it showed up.

The trouble was (even when I was attending to the world around me), I was still trying to eke things out of life, and therefore applied small digging and sifting tools to each moment. No matter what, I still couldn't leave it be much of the time. Instead, I (like most of us) tried to bend each experience to yield up a nugget—of happiness, of affirmation, of safety. I picked, or pick-axed, constantly.

Once, at a holiday gathering with close friends, I watched how each of us tried to sculpt the experience one way or another. One woman characteristically tried to mold the evening into a banter-and-laugh situation and, to that end, made one slightly off-color joke after another. She was running counter to a man trying to evoke the spiritual components of the meal—and attempting to make sure that everyone there understood how broad-minded and open his approach to spirituality was. Someone else applied conversational patches between the two approaches to ensure conviviality. And truly, it was a lovely evening.

But I couldn't help noticing the compulsive messing with the shape of the moment to which we all fell victim. What would have happened if our social anxieties had been held at bay? If we had trusted each moment enough to see what would disgorge? I noticed how deep was our/my distrust that the moment could safely be let alone—at least among a group of friends—and that what would emerge might be at least okay, if not way better.

Once, in a long conversation with Adyashanti, I described the ways my habitual editorial impulse—useful in my work in publishing—simply could not rest. I always assessed each moment of my life from the editorial stance: a bit of dialog was unnecessary;

surely an extraneous story line could get cut; and couldn't things get to the point already? You see, I said to him ruefully, it's built in. I want to massage each moment into *my* idea of beauty, or succinctness, or tone. It's so hard to let things be as they are. Trying to edit the way the world unfolds is obviously a losing game. He simply laughed and looked at me kindly.

Chased by Hell

I'm convinced that we are being drawn, by the best kind of magnet, towards our Fullness. It's always inducing us towards it, using every kind of circumstance—seduction, promises, pain, despair, ecstasy—whatever is needed next to prod us to let go of the debris we are clinging to along the way. And sometimes, when we're particularly obtuse, the prods hurt. A lot.

Over the course of a few weeks, a few years after the workshops with He Who Knows, a mysterious and severe pelvic pain took me from being a hiker and dancer to being someone who lay on the couch in extreme pain. It was the kind of pain that overrode my usual escapes: my books, my movies, my cogitations. I was scared; this disability brought up demons in my psyche that I hoped had retired to warmer climes long ago.

Strangely—or not—a week before I had any signs of this disease, I had a vivid dream in which I was told that hell beings were chasing me. It was odd: I so rarely remembered dreams, and those I did recall were mostly benign and banal. I wrote the message down in my notebook and promptly forgot about it. It was only months later that I remembered the dream and began to wonder if it had been not just symbolic, but terrifyingly factual. Demons, hell beings, or just ordinary physical breakdown, it was agony.

Two years before I became so disabled, a Tibetan lama known particularly for his clairvoyance and intuition came to my house for lunch.

I'd been inveigled into hosting this meal by a friend of mine—a devotee of the lama—who didn't have a nearby place of her own to lay out a comfortable lunch. I was looking forward to meeting the Tibetan master; I'm always curious about highly developed humans, how they are the way they are. So there we were, my friend and I, soup made and the house tidy.

The lama was in his eighties, but looked around fifty. There was not a wrinkle on his rosy face. Stepping carefully through the front door, he took my hand warmly, looked at me appraisingly, and asked me about my health. This was not politeness. Considering the difficulty of speaking through a translator—a young man trailing him— he wasn't the type to waste effort on irrelevant pleasantries. This was a pointed question, sharp and poky and burrowing into my gut.

He then went on to recommend a meditation practice, noting that it was helpful to develop it in order to deal well with pain. I didn't currently have pain. Then he recommended several times that I go see a doctor.

By the time lunch was over my throat was hurting. And as soon as my guests left and I could drop the social persona, I realized I was suppressing a spigotful of tears. The lama's implication that I had the kind of physical condition that warrants a timely consult with a physician—and furthermore that might bring me significant pain—had shocked me.

It felt like death was jumping out from behind the lama, poking out his tongue and rolling his eyes. I was shaken.

Two weeks later I developed a sudden, unremitting esophageal burning, severe enough to send me to a gastroenterologist. He was a pale pumpkin of a man, with a boyish flop of graying hair falling over one eye. He listened gravely to my tale. "Cancer," he said. Actually he didn't use the C-word, but a creative locution that made it absolutely clear what he meant. I wish I could remember exactly what words he used, but I promptly suppressed them.

He held up one small hand and ticked off the reasons he thought I had cancer, one for each finger. Five reasons. "On the other hand," he said, "these are reasons that weigh against 'it'." He enumerated them on his thumb and forefinger. Two reasons. The simplicity of the math made it worse.

"How fortunate," he said, without inflection, "I have a cancellation tomorrow. We'll put a camera down your esophagus and take a look." And then he ran out of the room.

"Are you really just going to walk away after telling me you think I have cancer?" I yelped at his white-coated back. He paused for a moment, and then kept going. The door closed.

Back at home I wept sporadically for hours. And then—to use the standard phrase—I put my papers in order. This was serious. I was going to die.

Esophageal cancer is a particularly nasty way to go, with its tendency to constrict one's breathing. But in the midst of my weeping, a part of me was intrigued to notice that the rest of me was grieving, but was not devastated. Perhaps, after all, my many near misses with death—and there were many— had actually had their effect. Death be not proud: I'm scared of you but no longer scared shitless.

And though I was scared, I was also interested. The digestive tract lends itself so generously to metaphorical use; it's so useful for describing withholding and over-sensitivity, acceptance and rejection and discrimination, and so much more.

But I was saved from having to burrow deeply into all this imagery—it turned out that my esophagus looked completely normal. This was a relief for the psyche but not for the body, not for a while. But eventually the pain faded, not to return.

And what of the prognosticatory lama? Before he left my house I pulled my friend aside. "He's freaking me out," I said. "Did he ever volunteer anything about your future health to you?" "No, never," she said.

The odd thing is that for the first few years after that time, I had little pain—other than the esophageal episode—while my friend developed one excruciating agony after another: a broken collar bone, serial migraines, a car accident, a fall that fractured three of her four limbs, and so on. I didn't have the heart to bring this issue up as a curious object of inquiry—she was so devoted to this guru. A few years later she was officially disabled because of pain. And now, after several years' delay, I had joined her.

Now when she came to visit we both reclined, one each of the two sofas in my living room. We talked about how to wrap our minds around the possibility that we might never feel better than we did at that moment. I was in pain—finally—and was terrified that this, this terrifyingly mysterious illness, was what the lama was talking about.

The inevitability of old age, sickness, and death is a favorite theme of Buddhists, who harp on its facthood endlessly. Why the endless repetition, I used to think; it's not like people don't know what's coming. But we don't really, or I didn't. There's nothing like a serious illness to get you real about what you truly believe, what you've really learned about the spiritual life. The issue gets acute; this is where the rubber hits the bitumen.

Initially I was shocked and indignant that this disability had happened to me—as though I should be granted some special immunity. Disability and death are supposed to come, I knew, but later, much later, surely.

I could see now that every time I'd had another close escape from the series of serious illnesses that had stalked me in my life, I had immediately repressed their horrifying possibilities. No wonder there were fermentations and eruptions of terror that let loose in my psyche now and then.

But this time I had to deal with it; the pain was impinging on my every moment. Discomfort was apparently my curriculum, devised by a school board who apparently believed that if you spare the rod you spoil the child or some such severe pedagogical viewpoint.

Which leads me to a description of my ailment:

One night, as we ladled a chunky stew onto our plates, Jeff turned to me. "So how are you feeling?"

"Do you want me to tell you now? Over dinner? It's going to be an X-rated version."

He nodded yes.

"It feels like someone perverse has put a TV remote up my butt and an old-fashioned telephone in my vagina," I began. (And yes, the moment after I said it, I noticed that both of these were objects designed to facilitate the delivering of information.)

Jeff put down his fork.

And those were just some of the symptoms, but perhaps the most interesting (to others) of the lot. My feet and hands cramped, I felt bands strangling my right thigh. My pelvic floor would spasm as though it were struggling to eject a fetus. I was in so much pain that I could no longer sit, nor could I stand still for more than a few seconds.

Of course, I could no longer have much of a social life; I'd never before realized how much of social interaction involved sitting. No more movie theaters, restaurants, or convivial dinner parties for me. No plane travel. No driving. My life, as I was used to living it, was shriveling rapidly around me.

Meanwhile, fruitless diagnostics continued. After six MRIs, I moved on to my next adventure: a spinal tap. Lumbar puncture. "It's a terrible name, isn't it," said my neurologist conversationally as she prepared to pierce my spine. "I always ask my patients if they can come up with a better one." It was a good gambit, but I didn't bite. I chose rather to say a mantra—*om mani padme hum, om mani padme hum, ommanipadmehum.*

And, really, Lovely Neurologist was highly skilled, because the procedure hurt less than receiving a filling.

She began to rhapsodize somewhere over my shoulder. "Oh, what beautiful spinal fluid!" she said and her enthusiasm didn't sound fake. "Beautiful."

I turned my head carefully. "Would you like to see?" she asked.

Indeed. And she held up three vials of clear liquid. It was crystalline, astonishing. I found myself unexpectedly moved. This was an intimate, hidden part of me, clear and adamantine. "Cool," I said, "that's really cool."

"People always expect that everything inside the body is green or yellowish," she said, "but look at this." She was thrilled and I was beyond thrilled. This previously unseen clarity deep within in me was the most obvious, unexpected metaphor. It buoyed me for days.

Disability Blues, Blacks, and Greys

I suspected that I was the current cautionary tale told among my acquaintances, the "there but for the Grace of God go I" example. When people saw me, I imagined they crossed themselves (or the equivalent) and hurried by. As in: Oh God, let it be her, not me.

I understood their sentiments. Despite my Buddhist mouthings about taking on others' suffering, I would rather that this had happened to a distant someone else.

The pain levels increased so much that for some time I couldn't comfortably lie on my back—which meant no reading. Which meant losing my favorite, most reliable distraction. My life now consisted of a deeply uncomfortable pacing the whole day inside the house, trying to handle the pain and burning. After a few hours I would be so tired; all I wanted was rest. But the demons pointed out that lying down would simply bring more pain. Keep walking, honey; that's the nature of this hell.

I was frightened that this strange life was my new status quo. Theoretically I could live several more decades. Could I really bear twenty or thirty years of not being able to sit down to dinner? I had to walk around in the house when I ate, holding the plate in one hand and fork in the other. It made for an uncultured quick shoveling of the food, in order to get the uncomfortable process over with. Twenty years without sharing a meal with friends, going out to a movie, or driving myself anywhere—all of which require sitting. Twenty years of alternating an agitated pacing with lying flat on my back. Twenty years of longing for bedtime and the relief from pain that my sleep medications brought. Twenty years of horribly intimate pain.

During this period I received an unexpected confession from a middle-aged acquaintance. "Competitive," he complained. "I'm still so competitive." Where he stands in the local scrabble rankings or among the gym denizens who can bench press more than a hundred pounds is still much too important for him, he said. In response I told him my humiliations, to help him—maybe—put such things into perspective.

"When I crawl on my hands and knees out of the back seat of the car, people avert their eyes because they know it's rude to stare," I told him. "It's strange to be the person that people pity—or simply think is weird." And I was now (I felt) a resented and resentful awkwardness at parties, laid out in a peripheral area, evoking obligatory kindnesses.

I was trying to tell him, Let it go before life forces you. But of course he couldn't hear me really. And who can make shifts like that, just from observing another's withering? Obviously I hadn't made those shifts; I was still being withered.

Yes, I knew that many people have it worse. At least I could get to the bathroom, wipe my own butt. I could rummage in the fridge. Truly, I was grateful. I now understood how quickly those acts of independence could be removed by a new regime coming into power. Yet secretly, with shame, I wished my condition were terminal: at least then I'd know that my suffering had an expiration date. It was a terrible thought, but that's how bad things were.

Old Anger

Ordinarily—despite my experience with the prognosticatory lama— I try to dismiss suggestions about my health that are offered by anyone claiming to use clairvoyant perception. I know that my own perceptions are often wildly off, and I'm pretty sure others are giving me strange mixtures of their own sticky psychological states with perhaps a viscous dab of truth.

But I was desperate, and so sometimes I listened perhaps more than I should have to any proffered occultly-mediated opinions.

As he worked on my spine, a chiropractor said he thought my illness had to do with something that happened to me as a child that made me very angry. He described me as he saw me: a young child, petulant and furious.

His suggestion would have gone straight into the dustbin of my mind except that five months beforehand a healer in Arizona, working on me at the very beginnings of the illness, had said the same thing. She gently inquired about what had made me so angry as a child, and suggested that my illness was intimately tied up with that event.

Well, the second query finally got my attention. I knew exactly what had made me angry as a child.

"The doctor says you're allergic to Daddy," said my mother one day when I was six. What?

A few days before this astonishing announcement my mother had taken me to see an allergist because I always seemed to have a runny nose. The man seemed austere in his elegant office in a prestigious neighborhood in Sydney.

This specialist determined, through abstruse means, that my chief allergy was to my father. It was suggested that, since a runny nose is apparently a terrible thing, I should stay far away from my dad. Boarding school seemed like the obvious solution.

Not any boarding school, but one deep in the mountains. A school close to home—there were several quite good ones—was not chosen, even though enrolling in one of these would have allowed at least my mother to see me frequently.

As I remember it, my school was modeled on the German-British idea that it was good to toughen kids up. Lack of heat, forced consumption of blackened, burnt porridge for breakfast, and scratchy wool underpants were all part of the regime, with even scratchier white wool underwear mandated for Sundays.

It was in the school's puddly playgrounds that I first saw ice in its natural habitat, outside the confinement of a freezer. A cold sheet was miraculously floating on a small lake of mud when I went outside one morning. Following the lead of the other girls (I was the youngest in the school) I picked up a piece and smashed it, hard, against the ground.

The cafeteria food was the Australian-British version of abominable: shepherd's pie, glutinous porridge, and the like. The highlight was jello for dessert on Sundays—a treat to which I looked forward to all week. Once when my parents came to visit—my father sitting at a separate booth in the local restaurant so as not to provoke my allergies—I begged to be returned to school so that I wouldn't miss jello. Alarmed by my priorities, my parents mollified me by immediately ordering me ice cream. Perhaps that was the moment when they decided that it might be good to bring me home.

Or perhaps it was something else. I was assigned to sleep in a large room lined with beds, each of them with iron bars for a headboard. After the lights were turned out, promptly at 8 PM, we children were not supposed to get out of bed. Visits to the bathroom involved an intimidating set of rule-breaking moves that I didn't quite understand.

One night, my bowels in turmoil, I let go into the scratchy underwear. Now I had a problem. Sitting up in the dark, I carefully pulled my woolly underpants and dropped them, contents and all, behind the iron bars on my bed. A few days later, faced with a similar bowel situation, I did the same thing.

Shortly after that my parents decided to withdraw me from that school.

No one ever said a word about my rather extreme acting out. I can only assume the school authorities strongly suggested to my parents that they take me home. Whatever happened, I was grateful to be back with my family.

Suddenly the issue of being allergic to my father seemed moot. Not a word was said about it, and we resumed our usual levels of proximity. The drippy nose didn't seem to be a major problem after all.

But all was not well. I was very, very angry.

I was never the kind of person who yells, strikes, or breaks handy objects. Instead, I turned into the kind of person who uses language—very cautiously—as weaponry.

After my boarding school experience, I figured that maybe something I'd said to my parents had caused them to discard me into what felt like a wilderness. (Even at six I knew that the drippy nose story just didn't make sense.) I had learned that you can think you're cherished and safe—but one day, for whatever reason, you can be sent away, discarded. Like trash.

Just saying what I thought—without editing—was now too risky. But I instinctively understood that I could use my voice as a modulated tool—comb, stiletto, wheedler—depending on what the situation called for.

The voice is a sophisticated bit of gadgetry. What it does can counteract the bad outfit at a job interview or, alternatively, nullify the perfect resume. But like all powerful tools kept at half-throttle, sometimes it just wants to let loose and shake down the walls of Jericho or sing Puccini. Actually it wants to be a full-body experience, with the lips and the tongue just forming the rosettes as the words and songs come barreling up from an array of abdominal organs.

Of course, I didn't know that then. It took me years to get back to partial throttle (with helpful prompting), but in the meantime, I knew I could take my revenge on my parents for what I saw as their betrayal—without being a disobedient girl—simply by the way I said things.

I began to use a natural talent for logic and debate to back my parents into indefensible and obviously contradictory stands on all sorts of issues, most of them quite unimportant to any of us. It was just my way of temporarily pulling the plug on their power. My father would shake his head, "You'd be a good attorney," he'd say, gamely.

But back to the body workers, and my anger. What more could it want of me? A primal scream of rage? A furious letter—written, burned, and its ashes scattered on the same plot of scrub where my parents' ashes had already been incorporated into saplings?

Grown-up Christi didn't think she was angry at all. Grown-up Christi understood that maybe my mother was in crisis back then, with one or other of her nerves breaking down; perhaps the allergy thing was possibly just an excuse to remove me while she recuperated. On the other hand the craziness about being allergic to my father was extreme. I mean, no one would make that up. Would they?

Seeing how deeply I must have buried my anger—so deep that I'd lost track of it—made me aware that I had an over-muscled internal enforcer, a fellow who did this work when I wasn't watching. What he didn't seem to get was that the problems he'd forced into some corner didn't simply curl up for a nap. Instead, they eventually fomented rebellions, employing slash and burn techniques which were managing to cause me pain.

So, I dutifully and hopefully felt my way to some of those cellars in which I'd tucked my anger, pried open small doorways, and let myself yell and scream. It felt good and cleansing and necessary, but—damn it—the pain obstinately persisted. Something more was apparently required.

The Shaft of Light

Okay, I thought. I have to move off the regular space-time matrix and bring in another dimension: the Holy. There was nothing else that could possibly make my life bearable. Now I regretted having shut down—so many decades ago—my understanding that I was an awareness having a dream or holographic experience. I had been way too successful in my attempt to buy into consensus reality, and now I couldn't easily return my purchase.

Nevertheless, after some experimentation, I discovered that the exercise that lead to my first breakthrough experience back with Anthony was the practice that helped me most in times of the fierce panic than arose as the level of pain accelerated. *Who is it that is knowing this experience?* I asked myself. And then reminded myself: *I am the knower, the awareness*. Everything that was happening—my pain, the bird outside, the kettle whistling—was simply a content within my awareness. As long as I could identify—even a little—with the awareness, things were bearable. The feelings would fade like overexposed film in the light of a dispassionate attention.

But the moment I stopped the practice—and it was impossible to keep it up all day—I'd crash into an acrid despair or be swallowed by panic. And so I prayed.

On days when I felt particularly trapped and frightened that I would never get better, I thought of the Dalai Lama descending out of the expanse of the world and materializing in my personal space, back in 1979. The Holy can show up, it seems, against all apparent odds, as a miracle or a visitation. Grace happens. Why not now?

God is chasing me, here, I thought. As in: *So, obstinate creature, you refuse to actually do real practice? After everything we've given you, everything you know? That's a fairly easy fix, you know. Are you listening? No? Ok, then.*

And so, pain and panic; they were forcing me to meditate and pray far more than I had before. And though I wasn't yet practicing as though my hair was on fire (as the Buddhists so colorfully recommend), I was praying as though my pelvis was pierced by a sword.

After an attempt at love-making—the technique amended by the necessities of my current condition—Jeff sighed happily. "You sexy thing," he said. He winked.

Some sex object. I thought that my naked body looked better than it had in decades; severe pain had eradicated my appetite and fifteen pounds. But sexual pleasure seemed horribly, drastically impossible. After all, that entire area was the source of much of the pain I experienced. It made me wonder if I was being punished in some specific way for a sexual transgression. But I couldn't remember any sexual transgressions—not this life, anyway. No affairs, no dangerous sex. I had been a tame, domesticated animal.

But PB had once suggested that, in a previous life, I was an over-sexed monk struggling with a level of desire that made an absurdity of a nominally celibate life style. I couldn't help but wonder if this pain of my nether regions was a stern correction, so that in future lives I'd have some level of trauma-driven caution around the perineal areas. The thought was so repressed-punitive-Christian, of the *mea culpa* variety, that I hoped it was not true. But true or not, I imagined that things would never be the same.

As to looking good, others did not agree. A good friend told me that I looked anorexic. She scolded me, like an anxious mother. I cried for days every time I remembered her words; it seemed too hard to have to worry about this, too—that I not only felt bad, I also looked bad—at least to her.

Another close friend—for years I spent time with her at least once a week and often more—abruptly moved on with her life. New friends, new activities. No time for me any more, now that I couldn't go dancing with her, or to concerts, or on hikes. Worse than that, she tried to convince other friends not to visit me, because doing so was "enabling" me. If abandonment was "good" for me, then who could blame her for ditching me?

I could. I was being discarded yet again by someone whose love I trusted. In previous years she had avowed, many times, that we were like family. Now months would go by without hearing from her. Hurt, hurt, hurt.

In *The New York Times* I found an article that spoke about the disappearance of friends during health crises. It's common, it seems. And when the writer of the article called out the ubiquitous "Let me know if there's anything I can do" as the uselessly vague offer that it is, I felt delightfully vindicated in my frustration with those who said that to me. On the phone I unkindly snarked at a semi-disappeared friend who told me that because he and his wife worried about me, I was not alone. D- for torqued logic, I thought. "Actions speak louder than a thousand worried words," I said tartly. He pretended not to hear.

Meanwhile other friends stepped forward, phoning me every day, visiting several times a week, offering extraordinary body/spirit work, calling from supermarkets to see if there's anything they could pick up for me.

Their kindness shamed me. I had not always shown up for people in the way I would have liked them to show up for me. If I got well, I swore, I would try to be a support to others. It's the usual cry of the pained: I'll be a better person, I promise. But I knew I would. Now I understood.

An old friend mentioned the Fisher King to me, a character that shows up in Arthurian legends, in Wagnerian operas, and in Jeff Bridges movies. The stories about him vary, but what is invariable is that he has a wound that will not heal—at least not until someone of sufficient purity can accomplish a specific task. In many versions, the king's wounds are in his sex organs and/or his legs—rather like mine. Unnervingly like mine—but that's where the similarities end. Unlike me, he is the keeper of the Holy Grail. The Grail, I gather, is the cup that caught Christ's blood as it dripped from him after he was on the cross. It's hard to imagine that someone was collecting his blood, but this is the stuff of myth and symbolism.

The Grail, like any cup, is a feminine object, a receiver of input. It seems to be a symbol of the feminine aspects of the Holy Spirit, as opposed to the Divine Spear with which it is often linked. King Arthur and his knights spent their lives searching for the Grail; it was their version of the search for the Holy.

But what about the wounded Grail-keeper? I wanted to know what it is about the responsibility of holding the Feminine Holy that keeps one wounded? One early version of the myth says that the Grail-keeper received his wound because he failed to unveil the Grail daily. Guilty, guilty, guilty. I didn't unveil holiness in any form on a daily basis. I didn't because I couldn't, didn't know how.

Practice like your hair is on fire. What the Buddhists mean is: Muster as much emergency action about finding the truth of your being as you would stamping out flames in your hair. I could see clearly that my life was burning away, that my days of being functional might be very limited. But somehow it was difficult to apply myself to much of anything. My capacity to concentrate for more than a few seconds had shriveled eerily. Perhaps this is a known side-effect of pain. I was hoping it was; then perhaps I wouldn't feel so guilty.

But guilt was only a minor player in my pantheon of negative thoughts that were beginning to wear me down. There were no more specialists to consult and thus, I thought, there was no more hope of a fix. If this constricted life of constant suffering, for possibly decades more, was my fate, I didn't want it. A voice within me was urging suicide. Secretly, seriously. I knew better, and yet thoughts of it rose up like an attack on my sanity. I fought them off the best that I could. And yet they were seductive.

On a very anxious day—one where thoughts of the Ultimate Escape tempted me more than they should—something brought a completely unexpected message in response.

Trying to distract myself, I went walking along a curving path by a lake. The beauty was so extreme that I kept taking photos with my cell phone. After each shot I'd return the phone to the pocket of my down coat, only to remove it moments later for another shot of a red lighthouse against the chopping water or a spectrum of leaves on a young tree.

Seeing yet another must-have view I pulled my phone out of my pocket again. On its screen, instead of the camera app, were the words Anthony Damiani. It was a double, triple-take moment for me. My thought processes juggled to try to understand that I was really seeing what I was seeing.

Yes, it most definitely said Anthony Damiani, right there in my e-mail contact list—even though I had not left that program open, and even though he had died long before cell phones and their contact lists existed. It felt like I was getting a text message from the ghostly realms.

Later that day I received a follow-up.

After the long walk I went home to rest, settling into my usual spot on the living room sofa. Jeff was working on a project in his study. A mere five minutes after I lay down he walked over to me and silently handed me a piece of paper.

"What?" I said.

"Look," he answered. "It just fell out of some old books I was moving."

On the wrinkled paper was a typed poem that Anthony had written, perhaps forty years beforehand. It was a prayer that ended with the lines:

teach me to surrender

Oh thou Unknown God -

have mercy, have mercy.

Surrender, not suicide. That was the message. The hell-beings temporarily foiled. Damn and hallelujah.

Surrender. I was beginning to see that the series of severe illnesses that have slapped me around my whole life must have been designed to finally bring me to my knees. In the sense of prayer; in the sense of not being able to stride around my life under the illusion of autonomy and potency.

I had to remind myself, over and over, that loss is normal. It's not necessarily that I screwed up. Or the Deity screwed up. Or the world screwed up. Like most of us, I took loss so personally, as though the universe were picking on me like some cosmic bully.

On the bad, self-pitying days I still wondered if a god had it in for me, the god in question being Jehovah, pal of Job. A god known for pushing to the limit: plagues, locusts, slaughters.

Of course, I knew better. This crisis—probably all my crises--was a sign that the divine (or my higher self) was taking me seriously when I begged so piteously to be spiritually infused. I'd prayed throughout the years to be shown the light, to be made awake to the holy.

You know the saying: Be careful what you ask for. But how are we to know that asking for a stream of divine love may mean wading first through acidic waters? The beatific gurus dispensing little samples of bliss—the first one's free, kids—didn't tell us. Or else we didn't listen, didn't really believe.

What's a responsible god supposed to do? He/she says (forgive the anthropomorphism): "OK, if that's what you want, let's do some major surgical reconstruction on every part of you that doesn't yet know its holiness. And let's face it: that's most of you." Of course it doesn't feel good. God doesn't use anesthesia.

This time around—this embarrassingly intimate pelvic disaster— I was being crushed like a walnut, smithereened, so that the only thing left to do was pray for the mercy of the same holiness that had dished this out.

One morning, as I lay there afraid, thinking what is there to look forward to this day, why bother, another thought bloomed so quietly that I almost missed it. And it was this: What if this is the day I get enlightened?

That changed things, not radically, but enough to temporarily take the edge off despair. And though I came no nearer to enlightenment that day, there were many joyful moments: paying attention to the touch of hot cocoa on my lip, sitting in the sun outside while Jeff puttered. Straight up, run-of-the mill mindfulness. Surely, surely, I could remember to do this every day? I could. It helped, but not enough.

A few days later, I turned on the TV simply to get away from my anxiety, and there was National Book Award-winner Barry Lopez. Lopez said two things that brought me to tears: *Despair is the great temptation.* And then he added something about "leaning into the light." I didn't hear it precisely, but what I heard was enough.

So, dear God, I prayed. Lead me not into temptation, and deliver me into the light. Despair (the voice of the hell-beings, I think) is seductive indeed; I had never been an optimist, even under the most stellar circumstances. And though I'd almost given up the thought that I could actually attain enlightenment or the light, merely leaning into it seemed like a surprisingly modest and possible goal.

Perhaps if I had an exoskeleton, like a lobster or a shell-creature, I could lean more deeply, I thought. The vulnerability of the human body—tender organs and nerves held within thin layers of skin—is appalling. The only reasonable thing to do was to give in, give over, to whatever was being delivered every moment, if only I could.

But gradually I did. I leaned into light, imagined as a shaft of holy brightness; something so literal was the best I could do. Also, I experimentally tried sending healing light to my pelvis. The result—at least, the immediate one—was astonishing. To my surprise, my lower spine immediately began a slight but insistent wave, a nudge, a shift, a realignment, and suddenly I was standing up much straighter than I ever remember doing before, no matter how much my mother nagged me—which she used to do frequently. When I invited it, the light shifted not only my body but my mood in small ways.

And I understood: this impossible-to-evade agony was forcing me *into* my body. If I stood a certain way, if I placed my weight exactly lined up with my middle toe, if I curved my back just so, the pain lessened. Perhaps if I'd been able to more fully occupy my body's real estate this way decades earlier, as PB had recommended, I wouldn't have needed this nasty lesson. True, my faith in the Holy's beneficence had briefly faltered in the face of what felt like a god-inspired cruelty. In the depths of my pain I had sometimes wondered what competent god would devise a universe that required so much suffering. But here I was; I had to deal with the local rules.

In any case, leaning towards the light was a beginning. Two years later, though I was still in pain, it was not the agonizing, I-want-to-die pain. Seven years later I could sit in a restaurant for a lengthy meal with friends. I was impaired, but I had my life back. I had been forced to lean on and into the light, the Holy, and my body and found that they not only kept me from falling but lifted me gently onto new ground.

Although I'd made it through this woeful part of my particular journey, I was ashamed at my apparent lack of fortitude. The hell beings (factual or metaphorical) had driven me unnervingly close to suicide; I suspected that they were related to the ones that PB noticed so long ago, coming back around for a second attempt at me when I was at my most susceptible.

Anthony helped save me, not only by the timely poem falling out of book, but also because he had told his students, long ago, that suicide is a really bad idea. It not only leaves one trapped in an in-between realm—according to occultists—unable to fully cross over for a long period, it also calls for a replay in a future life of the kinds of circumstances that caused one to check out early from this one. Apparently there really is no escape. I came through, shaken, and wanting Liberation, Awakening, more than ever.

Mr. Universe: Adyashanti

After my Mother Meera experience, I thought I was through with gurus and spiritual authorities of all kinds. Yet as I emerged from my years of extreme pain, I found myself paying particular attention to one teacher again, Adyashanti.

He was a short, shining man—Californian in the best and least woo-woo sense—who spoke of the spiritual search in ways I hadn't heard so clearly expressed before. The part of his message that initially hooked me was: At a certain point in the spiritual journey, it's best not to push so hard. What you seek is already present. *Allow* it, give it space to come forward.

Of course this was appealing. I'd so thoroughly failed at "breaking through" to Fullness/Emptiness despite my years of disciplined mental/emotional gymnastics. My spiritual work-out regimens, discontinued one by one, had included mantra, tantra, and so on—all of them based on the control-thought model of spiritual disciplines. All of them useful, more or less, but perhaps no longer quite right for my configuration at this point. That there might be another way was encouraging.

And I remembered that Paul Brunton had also suggested that this other approach was appropriate at a certain stage. PB calls this the short path, a direct approach that follows and works together with the long path, the very necessary path of discipline and self-improvement. The long path is the path described in most spiritual traditions, the one involving controlling the mind and body through practices, self-abnegation, and improving one's character.

In *The Short Path* (a posthumous compilation of his writings on the topic) Brunton explains that when one is ready, a direct turning to the Higher Self, a surrendering to it, a 180 degree turn, can be helpful. His description of this way is a little different than Adya's, yet close enough that Adya strongly endorsed that book.

It made sense now. My long path exercises had long ago run dry. It was time for a change.

A few years ago, Jeff and I spent over an hour chatting with Adya in a tiny gazebo overlooking a densely wooded valley. Jeff had been doing most of the talking, while I contentedly marinated in the potent energy field that always surrounds Adya. And then it was time to go. As we stood up, his name rang out loudly—apparently from my mouth—surprising all three of us.

"Look, Christi," he said, pulling me close. And he locked eyes with me and held the gaze for what seemed eons.

I knew he was trying to transmit something to me, give me an extraordinary opportunity, but my ego—which had been relatively quiescent for the previous hour—decided to shout and flail. *Do I look okay? Shut up. I'm blowing this. Shut uuup.* And so on.

Afterwards, as we sauntered up the hill, he was pleasant and warm, but I was castigating myself: How could I mess up this opportunity? It was embarrassing, humiliating. My damn ego had co-opted the whole situation, and was now working overtime. Yet again.

Two years later, I stood in a dusty parking lot outside a Tibetan Buddhist temple in Ithaca, awaiting Adya. Jeff and I had been asked to show him around Namgyal, the American outpost of the Dalai Lama's home monastery; it is an impressive complex of buildings, placed high on a hill overlooking Cayuga Lake.

After a few moments, a small Subaru pulled into an adjacent parking spot. The passenger door opened and out stepped Adya. For a moment I felt nothing—though I'd been actively trying to find my way into his short path practices, I hadn't actually seen him since his previous visit—and then something deeper in me again cried out loud, "Adya!" with so much force and implied exclamation points that I was briefly astonished before what came next displaced my surprise.

"I remember this face," he said warmly as he enfolded me in a hug. And there it was again: a deep, intentional connection through his eyes. Another chance.

Oh my god. His eyes were unlike any I'd seen before. How had I not noticed this last time? Afterwards I tried to fit words to the experience. Like looking into the sun. No. Like looking into the cosmic swirl of galaxies was more like it. They carried an energy beyond this solar system, it seemed to me.

Later, talking with a few friends who'd also had similar experiences when they'd had brief, close encounters with Adya's eyes, I realized that ocular energy transmissions, like this one, had been significant for me over the years: the Dalai Lama, Mother Meera. Whatever happens through the eyes can apparently change a life, had certainly changed mine.

So I decided to research the phenomenon, and quickly found this in Paul Brunton's *The Quest of the Overself:* "The adept or teacher initiates the aspirant...into the inner life of the Spirit merely by gazing deeply, intently and deliberately into his [or her] eyes for a few minutes....the adepts find the eye to be the only physical organ delicate enough and sensitive enough to be used as a medium of transmission and communication for their spiritual power."

It was a confirmation that I hadn't merely imagined all those experiences over the decades. I still didn't understand it, but perhaps I didn't need to.

Reading Adya and listening to his talks gradually transformed my whole approach to the spiritual path. His message is designed for people—like myself—who have learned through long experience that the will, useful as it is, cannot force open the gates to the holy. It can bring us right up close to those doorways, close enough to see (or not) that we are actually conjuring the barriers ourselves. Step back, says Adya. Drop your arms, let the gates fall.

But keep your gaze on the Divine. Listen within, attentively, he suggests. Don't grasp for a repeat of any spiritual "experiences" you may have had; if they were genuine, they have left traces within you. Locate the source of those traces.

And furthermore, he suggests that each of us ask ourselves the following: How am I avoiding the enlightenment that is always available in each moment? The moment we stop avoiding, the moment every bit of us thoroughly wants awakening, *no holds barred*, it happens.

His words touched a sensitive piece of scar tissue inside me. Yes, decades back I certainly had decided to smother my knowledge that I was my awareness and that the world I saw was not as solid as it presented. Over the years I'd thought I'd lost my opportunity, and that the opening I'd had then was gone, not to be repeated.

But listening to Adya I realized that of course the traces of what I "knew" must have left their mark. And that perhaps the realization that got curtailed, so long ago, might just be willing to come forward if I gave it a chance. I wasn't sure I was truly, deeply willing, but still.

When I first heard his approach, something in me relaxed, slightly. There was a quiet hallelujah of recognition. It made so much sense, right when I needed a compass needle to point me home.

Surrendering to Old Age and Everything Else, Maybe

At a convivial meal in an elegantish restaurant with Adya on the night after our tour of Namgyal, I started to choke on a limp piece of lettuce. As I stood up, hacking and sputtering, something in me thought, *Not a bad way to die, here with Adya*—and then the errant bit of salad dislodged and we resumed our meal. Calmly, Adya said the incident reminded him of his mother, who often choked during meals. He spoke of her lovingly, and then the conversation moved on. I remember the Grateful Dead were mentioned, and the discussion ricocheted around the table in a companionable way. It was the kind of chit-chat one doesn't remember afterwards.

Later, though, I thought, ah, now I'm old enough to remind a middle-aged someone of his mother (though I was not quite old enough to be Adya's). Apparently, I am an old person.

The first time it happened—the dire, self-redefining moment when I understood that I was perceived as old—I was unprepared. Wasn't I a gym-goer, a leanish creature? And that was just the physical. Wasn't I also a life-long spiritual practitioner who knew

(I thought) not to overvalue the brief dream of this world? Yeah, but.

Jeff and I had just boarded the subway on one of our many trips to New York City. A young Hispanic woman leaned over as our train pulled jerkily out of the station. "Please," she said, as she smoothly began to arise from a seat, "please, sit down."

Is she talking to me? O god, O Buddha, she is. "No, no," I said, motioning with my palm down for her to reverse and sit back down. She mistook my "no" for an appropriate, elderly politeness, and was now fully standing.

It would have been be too, too rude of me not to take the seat. I sat. "Thank you," I mouthed. What I meant was, thanks *a lot*, you've just told me that I look old.

It was over. The dream-ride of being a desirable female. Buddhist or not, I wasn't sure I was ready to let it go. Thank you, young woman, anyway; you're my subway-Buddha, dispensing an apparently needed lesson.

And part of me sighed with relief. I was being called to surrender to what is, yet again. I smiled at her, from the welcome comfort of the plastic seat. I was an old lady now, marveling at my elderliness.

So, I was aging visibly. And I had no one to blame, which was annoying. Whose fault could it possibly be? My indignation sputtered idiotically and uselessly, a train that had run out of rail.

It felt like the too-soon dawning of the age of dentures. Not long afterwards an old friend enthusiastically extolled the virtue of his high-end dentures. So we've come to this? The extolling of dentures? I'd confided to him my despair at the thought that one day I might have to remove a pair at night, transforming myself into a toothless crone for the delectation of my (horrified) husband, the teeth simmering in a stew of bubbling water on the bedside table. He was kindly trying to reassure me.

So I was crumbling. Dust to dust. Tooth enamel to denture. Hip or knee to titanium. Neuronal connection to Siri's circuitry. Rebuilding replaced by outsourcing.

It was the natural slow frog-boil of old age.

I thought of my father, who so easily accepted his aging. Although I had not succeeded in "helping" him with his spiritual life—PB's injunction to me—through me he had met the Dalai Lama and several other spiritual teachers. At least I could do that for him. In any case, he seemed like a fairly advanced being to me, kind and generous and ethical. And when Benji, Jeff, and I would see him in his last years, he'd take our hands. Swinging his thin arms back and forth, he'd chant, "Love, love, love," smiling joyfully. He had his own, perfect mantra, arisen spontaneously from who he was.

Enlightenment is absolute cooperation with the inevitable, says Adya. So far—obviously—I have not been able to consistently feel the contours of that kind of cooperation, but I truly have learned that the next moment will unfold any which way it damn feels like it. It's obvious, of course: There is nothing I can do to stop my aging, or an errant meteorite from crashing through the roof of my house, if the universe chooses to direct the latter improbable event towards me.

When I was younger I always expected space rocks, weather stations, whatever, to fall out of the sky: that is, a heavy, unyielding bit of unpleasantness plummeting toward me when I least anticipate it. Isn't that part of the psyche of every child of trauma survivors? Yet my life has shown me, repeatedly, that a stream of grace, a cornucopia of nectarous joy, might just as easily be flowing my way at any moment.

In either case, it's out of my control. I can relax a little around some of these things; I've been through the wash and spin cycle so many times that the fabric of my ego is getting thinner despite itself. So I'm old and wrinkled. That's just how it is.

It's all starting to feel acceptable, as is my death and the thought that I may not achieve enlightenment this lifetime.

I kept delaying finishing this book, praying for a good satisfying culminating experience that I imagined was expected by readers of this not-quite-memoir. Surely all those episodes, those contacts with spiritual leaders, are leading somewhere? Where is the turn around, the breakthrough, the enlightenment? The uplifting payoff?

And that, of course, is a terrible reason to hope for awakening. An embarrassingly egotistical reason. I knew that—for the sake of the authenticity of my spiritual life—I had to go ahead and finish my manuscript as it was, decouple my practice from my writerly ambitions.

Perhaps the most important thing that Adya taught me was patience when it comes to wanting enlightenment. Practicing like one's hair is on fire is fine if that kind of intensity is being demanded from within. But if it isn't, we can't fake it. And even if we try to fake it, what good will it do? Only when we are fully ready—and not before—can real enlightenment happen.

I can't force it, can't chase it down, can't capture it, just because my ego thinks it wants it. The poor thing has to let that ambition go too, along with everything else. Enlightenment is, after all, another thing the ego desires as an imagined enhancement. And, of course, awakening un-enhances the ego, revealing it as the slender, temporary collection of actions that it is.

At least I have identified those parts of me that hold back from awakening: they have provisos, such as, *only if I don't have to experience excruciating pain again, only if nothing bad has to happen to those I love*, and so on. My habit has been to try to flee the nasty vulnerability of embodiment, its unnerving susceptibility to suffering. Of course fleeing doesn't work; of course it causes problems of its own (such as psychic attack/anxiety). PB gave me my orders, back when I was twenty. Come in, be willing to experience embodiment, pain and all. Surrender to what is, because really, what choice do you have ultimately?

I now understand that if I really want enlightenment, I can't hold back. I have to be able to say—and mean it—*bring it on, no matter the price.* No bargaining. That's a sign of true surrender. I'm not there yet. Alas.

The vision PB gave me of my future development—so many decades back—showed me a little of what he saw: my fullest self, like a giant star with the best kind of gravity, pulling my battered, flimsy craft inexorably toward it. I'll get there eventually, when it's meant. In the meantime, the best I can do is try not to fight that tractor-beam, and look out the cockpit window in awe at this mystery.

Afterword

Apparently, the Answer, the Holy, wants to give itself. It's persistent, and endlessly creative in its attempt to get our attention. It cajoles us with bliss, impresses us with mystery and miracle, and—if it has to—bullies us with fear and pain.

Looking back over decades of attempting to live a spiritual life, I see that this truth has manifested in small ways over and over again. It's surprising, every time. I don't know why I'm so slow at really taking it in. I keep thinking I have to do all the wooing; and yet it's become clear that the interest lies on both sides.

Paul Brunton pointed this out to me, so long ago. Looking towards a beautiful painting on his wall depicting some otherworldly beings, he told me that we humans only have to take one step toward the holy in order for the holy to take ten steps towards us. I keep stepping forward, as I am able, thrilled—despite my clumsy stumbles—to be part of this strange cosmic dance.

To get in touch, or to read some of my articles, essays, and cogitations,

please visit my website:

christicox.com

Made in the USA
Coppell, TX
08 March 2021